Implementing SAP
with an ASAP methodology focus

Implementing SAP

with an ASAP methodology focus

Arshad Khan

Writers Club Press
San Jose New York Lincoln Shanghai

Implementing SAP
with an ASAP methodology focus

All Rights Reserved © 2002 by Arshad Khan

No part of this book may be reproduced or transmitted in any form or by any means, graphic, electronic, or mechanical, including photocopying, recording, taping, or by any information storage retrieval system, without the permission in writing from the publisher.

Writers Club Press
an imprint of iUniverse, Inc.

For information address:
iUniverse, Inc.
5220 S. 16th St., Suite 200
Lincoln, NE 68512
www.iuniverse.com

ISBN: 0-595-23398-8

Printed in the United States of America

"SAP" is a registered trademark of SAP Aktiengesellschaft, Systems, Applications and Products in Data Processing, Neurottstrasse 16, 69190 Waldorf, Germany. The publisher gratefully acknowledges SAP's kind permission to use its trademark in this publication. SAP AG is not the publisher of this book and is not responsible for it under any aspect of press law.

The following are some of SAP AG's trademarks (or registered trademarks), along with their corresponding descriptor and registration status, in the USA:
ABAP/4® programming language
ABAP™ programming language
Accelerated R/3™
AcceleratedSAP™ methodology
Accelerated <anything>™ software
ASAP™
EarlyWatch™ services
EnjoySAP™ initiative
mySAP.com™
R/2™
R/3™
Ready-to-Run R/3™
SAP™
SAPPHIRE® conference
SAP™ R/3® software
SAP™ R/2™ software
SAP APO™
SAP™ BW software
TeamSAP™ program

Contents

Introduction xxiii

Chapter 1: Need for enterprise resource planning software 1

Understanding ERP systems 1
    What an ERP system aims to do 1
    ERP objectives 1
    ERP evolution 2
    Components 2
    Is it all or none 2
    Main players 3

Why companies implement ERP systems 3
    Overcoming existing limitations 3
    Benefits of an ERP system 4
        Internal integration 5
        Process 5
        Flexibility 5
        Continuous improvement 5
        Reporting and information access 6
        Controls 6
        Costs 6
        Performance 6
        Technical 7
        Other 7

    Tangible benefits 7
    Cost savings 9
Challenges and problems with ERP systems 10
    Implementation cost 10
        Factors to be evaluated 10
        Cost estimation 11
    Consulting cost 11
    Total cost of ownership 12
    Implementation time 13
    Customization 14
    Inadequate preparation 14
    Fear of failure 14

Chapter 2: What is SAP 15

Background 15
    The company 15
    Main product 16
    SAP customers 16
Comparing implementation benefits 17
    Competitive implementation time 17
    Financial benefits 17
        Average benefits 17
        Example of specific benefits 17
Characteristics of SAP™ R/3® software 18
    Basic characteristics 18
        General 18
        Business 18
        Flexibility 19
        Technical 19
        Other features 19

Best business practices 19
   Industry-specific functionality 20
   Customization 21
      Need for customization 21
      How customization is done 21
      Complexity of customization 22
      Problem in customizing 22
Support provided by SAP 22
   TeamSAP™ approach 22
   Service and support 23
   Training 23

Chapter 3: Functionality and architecture 24

Functional architecture 24
   SAP modules 24
   Integration between modules 25
   Functionality by module 25
      Financial & Asset Accounting 25
      Controlling 26
      Investment Management 26
      Treasury 26
      Enterprise Controlling 26
      Real Estate 27
      Human Resources 27
      Plant Maintenance 27
      Production Planning 28
      Project System 28
      Quality Management 29
      Sales and Distribution 29
      Materials Management 29

Service Management	30
Business Processes	30
Basis Components	30

Physical architecture 30
- Three-tier client/server architecture 30
- Database layer 31
- Application layer 31
- Presentation layer 31
- Advantages of a decentralized system 32
- Platforms supported 33

Understanding SAP's environment 33
- Structural elements 34
  - Instance 34
  - Client 34
- Organizational structure 35
  - Client 35
  - Company code 35

Chapter 4: Impact of SAP implementations 37

Analyzing failures 37
- High profile failures 37
- Types of SAP project failures 38

Explaining failures 38
- Wrong software selection 38
- Inadequate planning 39
- Inadequate organization structure 39
- Lack of understanding 39
- Not appreciating implementation complexity 39
- Unable to understand implementation risks 40
- Being over ambitious 40
- Operating strategy did not drive business process design and deployment 41

  Rush to completion 41
  Not prepared to accept the new system 41
What SAP does to an organization 42
  Re-engineering 42
  Impacts corporate culture 42
  Changes competitive landscape 42
  Creates interdependency 42
  Shifts balance of power 43
  Simplifies platform 43
  Impacts costs/profitability 43
  Impacts employees 43
  Impacts work environment 44
  Provides flexibility 44
  Influences development 45

Chapter 5: Implementation methodologies 46

How SAP projects are implemented 46
  Basic essentials 46
  Implementation roadmap 46
  Big versus small approach 47
    Big bang approach 47
    Phased approach 48
Implementation methodologies 48
  Conventional methodology 48
  ASAP™ methodology 49
  Comparing conventional and ASAP™ methodologies 50

Chapter 6: ASAP™ methodology 51

Background and overview 51
  Need for ASAP™ 51
  What ASAP™ can do 52

How ASAP™ is implemented 52
ASAP™ implementation costs 53
When ASAP™ is not an appropriate choice 53
Current ASAP™ status 54

ASAP™ components and tools 54
Where can they be used 54
R/3™ Reference Model 54
Toolkit 55
Business Engineer 55
Project Estimator 56
Implementation Assistant 57
Question and Answer Database 58
Issues Database 58
ASAP™ Roadmap 58
Accelerators 59
Project Quality Check 60
EarlyWatch™ 60
Concept Check Tool 60

Chapter 7: Phase 1 - Project Preparation 62

Organizational readiness 62
Getting decision makers on board 62
Management tasks 62
Linking personal and project success 63

Project planning 63
Identifying critical elements 63
Guiding principles 64
Strategic guiding principles 64
Project business drivers 65
Budget, standards and metrics 65

Building the implementation team 66
    Organizational structure and project team authority 66
    Team membership 66
    Selecting consultants 67
    How teams are organized 68
    Team characteristics 68
    Team building 69
    Training for team members 69

Chapter 8: Phase 2 - Business Blueprint 70

Objective and scope 70
    Analyzing the business 70
    Interview objectives 70
    Reference scope document 71
    What the blueprint document contains 71
    Training for team members 72

Defining the organizational structure 72
    Organizational structure characteristics 72
    Impact of organizational structure 73
    Important elements of the organizational structure 74
        Company code 74
        Controlling area 74
        Business structure 75

Chapter 9: Phase 3 - Realization 76

Simulation 76
    Configuration 76
    Playbacks 77
    Other tasks 77

Validation 78
   Configuration 78
   Business process procedures 78
   End-user documentation 78
Unit and integration testing 79
   Need for testing 79
   Unit testing 80
   Integration testing 80
      Business scenarios 80
      End-user involvement 81
      Signoff 81
   Testing process 81
   Who does the testing 82
Data conversions 83
   Factors to consider 83
   Data migration methods 84
   When to start data migration 84
   Which data to migrate 84
      Automated master data 85
      Manual master data 85
      Automated transaction data 86
      Manual transaction data 86
   Data cleanup 86
      Why dirty data is an issue 86
      What cleanup involves 86
      Where is the data checked 87
      Who needs to validate migrated data 88
      Tools available 88
Interfaces, enhancements and reports 88
   Interfaces 88
   Enhancements 89
   Reports 89

Chapter 10: Phase 4 - Final Preparation 91

Preparing for the home stretch 91
   Refining the system 91
   Prepare go-live plan 92
      Cutover plan 92
      Important elements of the cutover plan 92
      Plan approval 93
Preparing the users and support staff 93
   How much to spend on training 93
   End-user training 93
      Why training is required 94
      Who needs to be trained 94
      Training scope and cost 94
      Training materials 95
      Time constraint 95
   Knowledge transfer 96
      Who should perform knowledge transfer 96
      Why knowledge transfer is ignored 96
      What needs to be done 97
Getting ready to throw the switch 97
   System administration 97
   Data migration 97
   Final testing and fine tuning 98

Chapter 11: Phase 5 - Go-Live & Support 99

Final check before take-off 99
   Readiness assessment 99
   Operational support 100
   Change controls 100
   Communication 100

Where it is required 100
What needs to be communicated 101
Security 102
Why security is required 102
How authorization profiles are created 102
Balancing security and access needs 103
SAP support 103
Online Service System 103
EarlyWatch™ 103

Thinking beyond go-live 104
Organization structure 104
Change control procedure 104
Staffing 105

Chapter 12: Project principles, guidelines and tips 106

Factors to consider before starting the project 106
Why is the project being undertaken 106
Project justification 107
Has the business strategy been defined 107
How will the SAP system be used 107
Readiness assessment 108
Skills assessment 108
Decision making capabilities 109
IT transition ability 109
Corporate culture 110
Management and implementation 110

Laying the foundations 111
Defining the guiding principles 111
Identifying the business drivers 111
Obtaining sponsorship 112
Obtaining management commitment 112

Recognizing the decision makers 112
Choosing the implementation leader 113

Chapter 13: Factors impacting project success 114

Planning 114
    Organization and management readiness 114
    Effective project planning 114
    Project team organization 115
        Organization of project teams 115
        Employees or consultants 115
    Project team characteristics 116
        Characteristics of team members 116
        Ability to think out of the box 116
Controls 117
    Effective controls 117
    Project manager's background 117
    Scope creep 118
        Understanding scope creep 118
        Setting rules 118
Technical 119
    Client architecture 119
        Impact of client architecture 119
        Undefined architecture 119
    Early start to data migration 120
    Thorough integration testing 120
    Data cleanup responsibility 121
Miscellaneous 122
    Responsibility and ownership 122
    Knowledge transfer 122
        Why transfer knowledge does not occur 122
        Repercussions of knowledge transfer failure 122
        Ensuring knowledge transfer 123

Effective communication 123
    Working in close proximity 123
    Promoting communication 123

Chapter 14: Tips for success 125

What should be done 125
Obtain commitment 125
Start moving quickly 125
Be prepared 126
Build team and end-user commitment 126
Create and maintain enthusiasm for the project 127
Solve problems in a timely and effective manner 128
Understand what can cause budget overruns 129
    Who should estimate costs 129
    Controlling costs 129
    Contingency 129
    Areas to watch 129
Build appreciation for inter-dependence 130
Emphasize thorough and effective testing 130
Start data migration early on 131
Create thorough documentation 132
    Training budget pruning 132
    Understanding documentation needs 132
    System reference documentation 132
    Ensuring successful documentation 133

What should not be done 133
Do not favor technology over business 133
Do not place functionality requirements on the back seat 134
Avoid duplicating old business processes 134
Do not ignore scope creep 134
Do not ignore risks 135

>   Do not modify the system unless necessary 135
>   Avoid changing standard R/3™ objects as much as possible ..136
>   Do not start development until requirements have been
>   established 136
>   Do not be bypassed 136
>   Do not let consultants loose 137
>   Do not underestimate end-user training needs 138
>   Do not ignore warning signs from partners 138

Common mistakes and pitfalls 138
>   Approach and analysis 138
>   Planning and control 139
>   Team leadership and characteristics 139
>   Scope 139
>   Data migration 139
>   Development and testing 139
>   Ownership and involvement 139
>   Customization 140
>   Consulting 140
>   Communication and training 140

Chapter 15: Influence of the marketplace on SAP 141

Future ERP growth expectations 141
>   ERP market growth rate 141
>   SAP growth drivers 142

Drivers for change 142
>   Internet 143
>   Supply chain management (SCM) 143
>   Customer relationship management (CRM) 144
>   e-Commerce 144

SAP's response to the rapidly changing environment 144
>   EnjoySAP™ 145
>   mySAP.com™ 145

Business intelligence 146
    SAP reporting limitations 147
    Data warehouse solution 147
    SAP™ Business Warehouse 147
Ready-to-Run R/3™ 148
    Components 148
    Features and benefits 149

Appendix: Evaluating ERP software 151

Prerequisites for ERP software selection 151
    Basic selection guidelines 151
    Use a proven methodology 151
    Evaluate the business strategy 152
    Study the business processes 152
    Evaluate the impact of a re-engineering decision 152
    Favor industry-specific templates 153
    Involve the business users 153
    Be wary of proof-of-concept offer 154
    Be aware of the cost of failure 154
    Additional points to ponder 154
Basic selection considerations 155
    Model of doing business 155
    Functionality 156
    Analysis and reporting 156
    Show stoppers 156
What to do before buying 157
    Evaluate using cross-functional teams 157
    Check references and sites 157
    Request onsite demo 158
    Beware of consultants involved in the selection process 158

Selection nuts and bolts 158
    Selection criteria 158
    Scoring and ranking ERP packages 160
        Scoring 160
        Ranking 162
    Vendor selection tips 163

Index 165

About the Author 173

Introduction

This book has been written with the objective of targeting professionals who plan to work on SAP, or other types of ERP, projects. It will be useful to a wide range of personnel including senior executives, directors, project managers and project implementation team members including functional/business analysts, developers and trainers.

The book covers a wide range of topics including the need for ERP software, SAP characteristics and functionality, and implementation methodologies. It extensively covers the five ASAP implementation methodology phases: Project Preparation, Business Blueprint, Realization, Final Preparation, and Go-Live & Support.

The book also covers project principles, guidelines and tips that are applicable to SAP implementations. It also discusses the trends that are expected to impact the growth of ERP systems in the future. Finally, a methodology for evaluating ERP software is described for those who may consider implementing an ERP system.

Every SAP and ERP software project implementation is unique. However, all such projects face many common problems, issues and risks—which have been identified or discussed at length in this book. For those who understand the unique nature and the challenges facing such projects, and take appropriate action during project implementation, the probability of success is increased considerably.

Chapter 1
Need for enterprise resource planning software

Understanding ERP systems

What an ERP system aims to do

An enterprise resource planning (ERP) system is a sophisticated software package that aims to run an organization's core business and major business processes. Typically, such a system supports and automates a company's business processes and functions such as order entry, procurement, finance, manufacturing, warehousing, shipping, human resources, etc.

An ERP system implies the use of an integrated and packaged, rather than customized, software developed for customers who can use it for most of their business needs. By providing integrated software, an ERP system eliminates complex and expensive links between different applications/systems that were never designed to talk to each other. While most ERP packages are developed for sale to customers, such functionality can also be developed in-house by companies. However, in such cases, the cost can be prohibitive besides being risky.

ERP objectives

There are many benefits to be gained by implementing an ERP system. However, the primary objectives for implementing such a system are:

- Enterprise-wide integration
- Fix broken processes
- Integrate vendors and customers
- Increase efficiency
- Gain competitive edge

ERP evolution

In the 1960's, most manufacturing systems focused on inventory control. In the 1970's, the focus shifted to materials requirement planning (MRP), which took into consideration master scheduling, raw materials planning and procurement. In the 1980's, this evolved into manufacturing resources planning (MRP II), which incorporated additional activities such as shop floor and distribution.

In the 1990's, more functionality continued to be incorporated including finance, human resources, project management, and engineering. The inclusion of these areas, which encompass the majority of the activities within a typical enterprise, led to the coining of the term enterprise resource planning (ERP).

Components

The different parts of an ERP system are referred to as modules—such as Finance, Project System and Materials Management. These modules can be modified and configured to reflect each company's unique business. Depending on the type of business, the ERP modules to be implemented by different companies can vary significantly. Finance is a universally implemented module, while Materials Management (MM) and Sales and Distribution (SD) are also widely used.

Is it all or none

In principle, an ERP system can operate independently without interfaces to an organization's own, or external, applications. However, in practice, most ERP systems require such interfaces, which enable information integration across the organization. Building interfaces requires varying degrees of effort. They can be built using the ERP vendor's proprietary tools or standard programming languages.

Main players

The leading ERP vendors are SAP, Oracle, PeopleSoft, JD Edwards, Baan, System Software Associates (SSA) and Lawson. According to AMR Research estimates, SAP AG was the ERP market leader with a 29% percent market shares in 2000. Both Oracle and PeopleSoft had a 17% share while JD Edwards trailed with a 6% market share[1].

Why companies implement ERP systems

Overcoming existing limitations

Since the early 1990's, American companies have been competing in an intensely competitive environment—both at home and abroad. The drive to cut costs, improve productivity, and stay ahead of the competition has been relentless. Every tool available to meet these objectives has been evaluated and, when appropriate, used.

Not surprisingly, information systems have always been identified among the most valuable tools that can help management achieve their performance improvement objectives. The reason for this is that corporate information systems provide the information that help businesses run efficiently and achieve their objectives. However, when management attempted to utilize the legacy non-ERP information systems for this purpose, it quickly became apparent that they had many limitations, such as:

---

[1] EC World, December 2000, pg 79

- Lack of integration because data was scattered across a variety of legacy systems
- Incompatibility between systems
- Inconsistent and/or redundant data
- Inability to provide real-time enterprise-wide information
- Inability to support easy consolidation of groups
- Limited scalability and upgrade limitations of existing systems (hardware, software and functionality)
- Integration problems for enterprise-wide upgrades
- Need to deal with multiple vendors
- High cost of maintenance due to disparate and obsolete systems

Benefits of an ERP system

The limitations of legacy information systems in meeting an organization's needs led to the search for a solution that would bypass their shortcomings. The aim was to provide a system capable of meeting a company's many divergent requirements through the use of a single program. The result of the search was the development of various integrated ERP systems. The typical benefits of an ERP system include:

Business
- Supports companies with global operations
- Accommodates rapidly changing business conditions
- Enables companies to better understand their business
- Meets customer demands involving multiple locations and interrelated items

Internal integration
- Integrates company-wide data and information
- Enables easy consolidation of groups due to availability of centralized data in one system
- Combines functions of many applications, that an organization needs to operate, and integrates them

Process
- Creates more efficient processes that serve customers better and maximizes profits
- Enables enterprises to standardize business processes and easily implement best business practices
- Provides access to best business practices, which are built-in

Flexibility
- Permits addition or upgrade of other system components or functionality due to open system architecture
- Any change can be implemented for all locations/groups through a configuration change at one central point
- Flexibility for changes for both business users and IT

Continuous improvement
- Supports the entire life cycle—not just the initial implementation
- Additional business processes can be implemented
- Can be used to optimize existing business processes

Reporting and information access
- ❑ Availability and easy access to transaction flows and document history
- ❑ Standard reports are available but customized reports can also be developed
- ❑ Provides drill down capability, i.e., access to detailed data

Controls
- ❑ Minimizes errors across various functions due to validity checks that are facilitated by an integrated system
- ❑ Provides an excellent audit trail
- ❑ Controls security through authorizations that can be maintained at different levels
- ❑ Enables easy corporate control and analysis

Costs
- ❑ Cost savings are realized (though few companies implement ERP for this reason)
- ❑ Easier and cheaper to maintain a single enterprise-wide system than a multitude of disparate, incompatible and obsolete applications/systems

Performance
- ❑ Creates a responsive and agile organization
- ❑ Enables performance of different groups to be compared easily due to a common standard format

Technical
- Provides real-time information
- Portable across operating systems, databases and presentation formats
- Provides high reliability

Other
- Supports extended supply chain management
- Improves return on information and return on investment (ROI)
- Facilitates efficient resource planning in a dynamic environment characterized by rapid changes in resource availability, plant capacity, etc.
- Reduces tedious jobs like matching purchase orders to invoices
- Provides user-friendly interface

Tangible benefits

ERP systems provide both intangible and tangible benefits. According to a Benchmarking Partners survey[2], maximum tangible benefits are provided by ERP systems in the following areas:
- Inventory reduction
- Personnel reductions
- Productivity improvements
- Order management improvements

---

[2]SAP Strategy Letter, April 26, 1999

The magnitude of these, and other, tangible benefits are shown graphically in Figure 1.

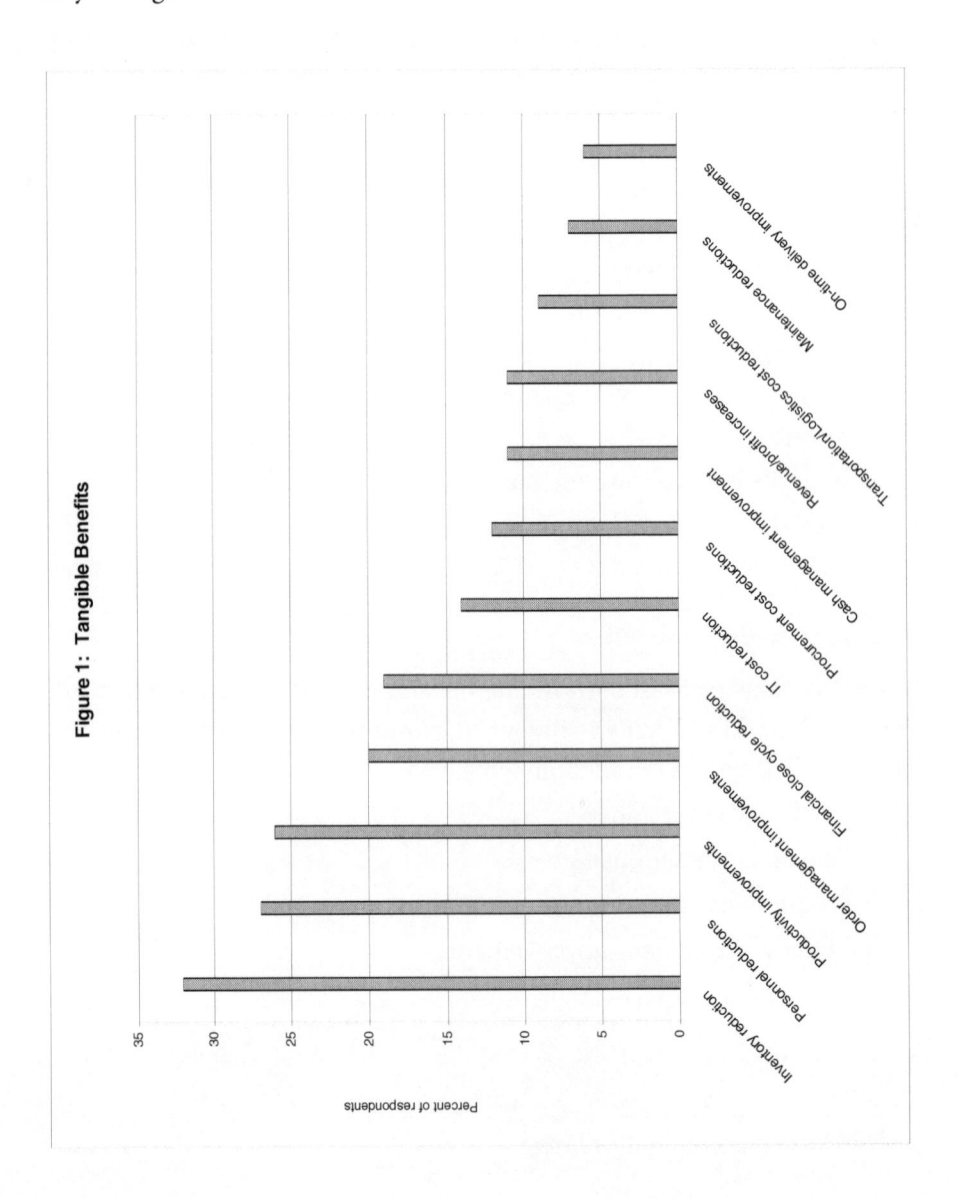

Figure 1: Tangible Benefits

Figure 2 indicates the quantifiable benefits associated with an ERP implementation as determined by the Benchmarking Partners survey. Fifty three companies reported cost attainment benefits while nine reported revenue attainment benefits.

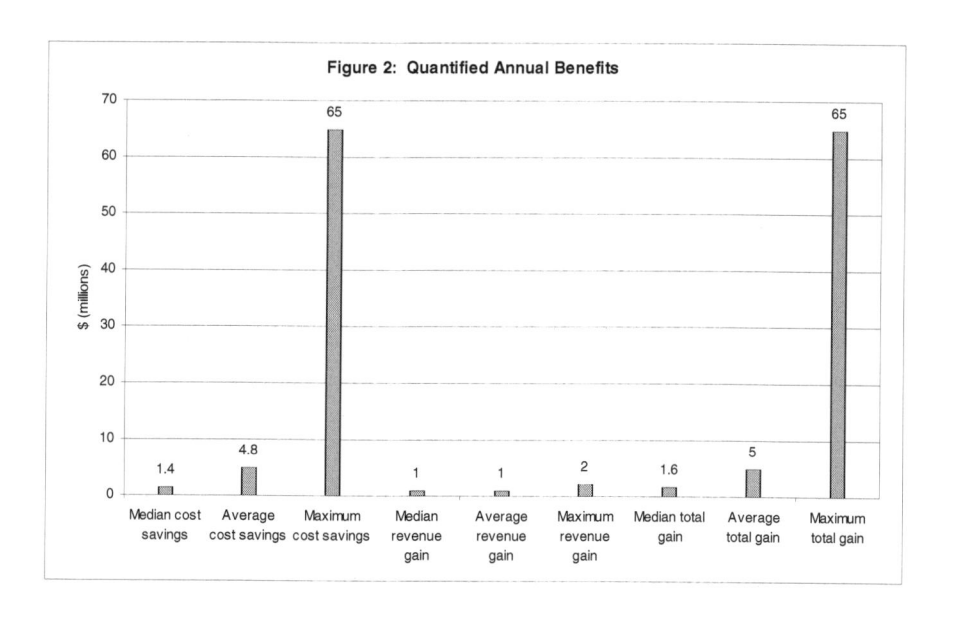

Figure 2: Quantified Annual Benefits

Category	$ (millions)
Median cost savings	1.4
Average cost savings	4.8
Maximum cost savings	65
Median revenue gain	1
Average revenue gain	1
Maximum revenue gain	2
Median total gain	1.6
Average total gain	5
Maximum total gain	65

Cost savings

The cost savings at each installation can vary tremendously. These depend on a number of variables such as the scope of work. According to a Meta Group survey conducted in 1999, based on 53 responding companies, the average annual savings from ERP implementations exceeded $5 million. The median annual savings was $1.6 million[3].

---

[3] SAP Strategy Letter, Volume 1, Number 4

Challenges and problems with ERP systems

All across the world, businesses have been implementing ERP systems as a cost efficient alternative to their disparate and incompatible systems that were put together over a number of years. While replacement ERP systems provide many benefits, as listed earlier, they also have some shortcomings. These limitations can become barriers to their selection and implementation, especially for small and mid-sized companies. Some of the major shortcomings are described in the following sections.

Implementation cost

The implementation cost of an ERP project is usually very high. Additional costs for consulting, integration and testing can be significant. Therefore, when the total implementation cost is calculated, a potential ERP investment can often be ruled out due to the huge cost involved. Hence, it becomes very important to estimate, as accurately as possible, the total cost of an implementation. This is a difficult task due to the large number of, and conflicting, factors that need to be considered for such an evaluation.

Factors to be evaluated

For each project, a different set of factors need to be evaluated. The reason for this is that no two enterprises are identical. There can be differences due to:

- Size
- Industry
- Number of corporate divisions
- Functionality to be implemented
- Existing (legacy) information systems
- Management style
- Corporate culture

- Method of doing business
- Processes
- Existing hardware and network infrastructure
- Number of users
- Other factors

Therefore, the scope and cost of every implementation will be different. Hence, it is usually not feasible to use other implementations as benchmarks for cost evaluation. Another problem faced by executives trying to compare a similar ERP implementation is the lack of cooperation by competitors. Most companies, especially competitors in the same type of business, will not share their cost figures for obvious reasons.

Cost estimation

One method used for cost estimation is based on estimating the total project cost as a multiple of the software cost. For example, one analyst estimates that the total cost of an ERP implementation ranges from 3-10 times the cost of the software. However, this rule-of-thumb is anything but widely accepted. A more widely used number is 3-5 times the cost of the software. Another benchmark is based on the cost per user.

In general, even though ERP projects have a higher overall cost than other software projects, they have a lower cost per user. This is due to the far larger number of users at ERP installations.

Consulting cost

Consulting costs can be very high for ERP projects. According to a June 1998 study by the Aberdeen Group, consulting fees at three SAP installations that used the AcceleratedSAP™ (ASAP) methodology accounted for 36% of the total project cost. However, these costs can be considerably higher for projects where excessive customization or business process re-engineering is performed.

Total cost of ownership

Due to the bigger organizations that have been implementing SAP, as well as being larger in scope, the total cost of ownership for SAP is the highest among the top ERP vendors, as shown in Figure 3.

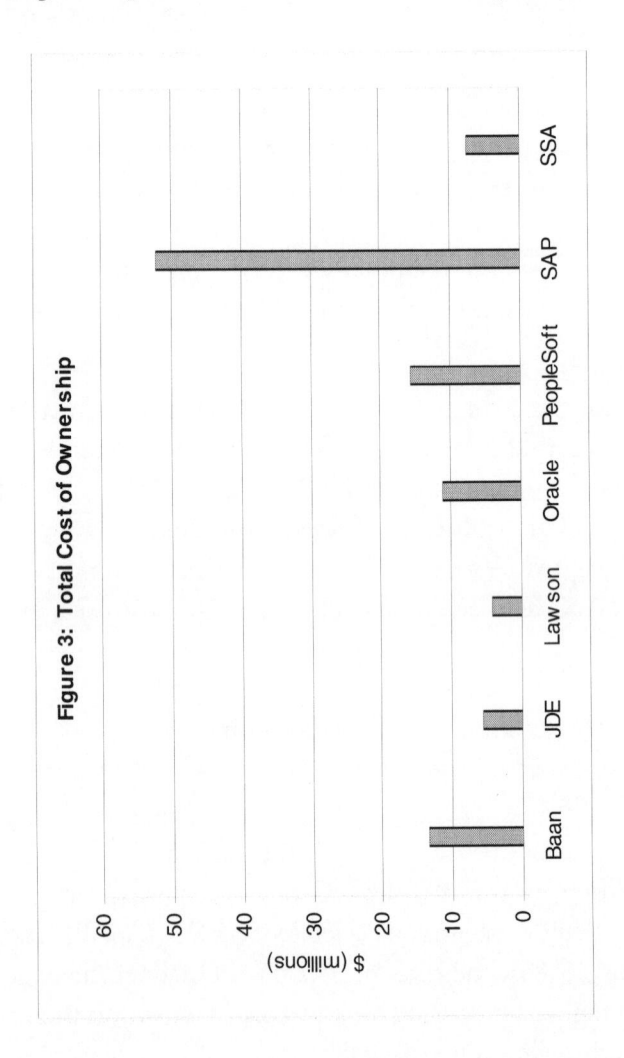

Figure 3: Total Cost of Ownership

Another metric for evaluating costs associated with implementing an ERP package turns up surprising results. According to the Meta Group, SAP has the second lowest total cost of ownership as a percentage of corporate revenues, as shown in Figure 4. It is the second lowest at 2.0% while its competitors, Baan at 3.4% and Oracle at 3.0%, are much higher.

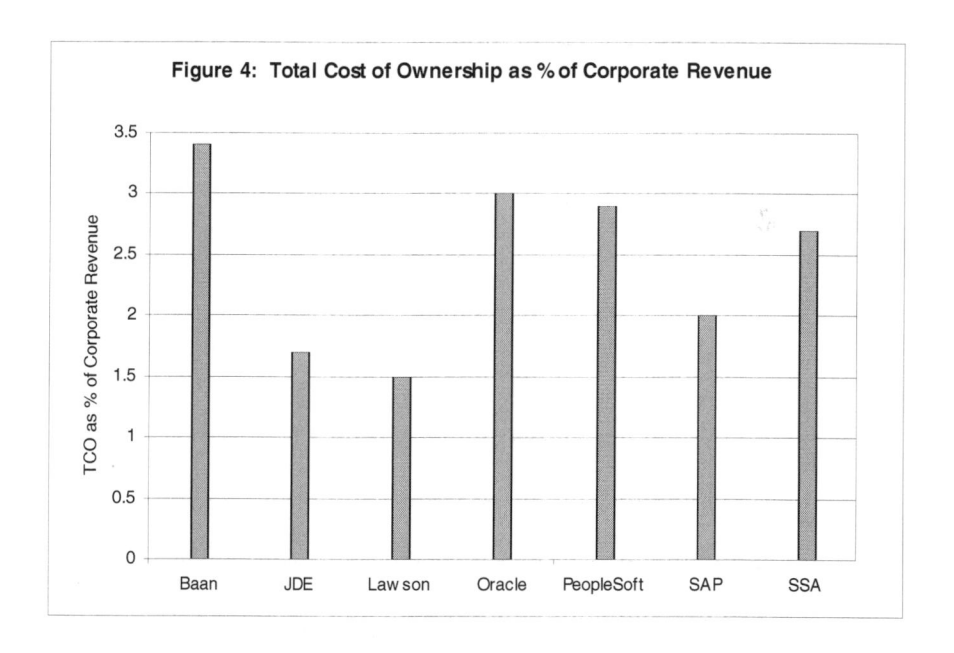

Figure 4: Total Cost of Ownership as % of Corporate Revenue

Vendor	TCO as % of Corporate Revenue
Baan	3.4
JDE	1.7
Lawson	1.5
Oracle	3.0
PeopleSoft	2.9
SAP	2.0
SSA	2.7

Implementation time

It used to take a very long time to implement ERP projects which seriously interfered with, and impacted, ongoing operations. A few years ago, it was not unusual for an ERP implementation to take 2-3 years. Delays were common and ERP projects got a bad name. However, in recent years, SAP projects have been implemented in a shorter time frame. This can be attributed to introduction of the ASAP™ methodology as well as experience gained from prior SAP implementations. While a typical ASAP™ implementation takes about a year, some projects have been completed within six months.

Customization

The need to tailor ERP software to the business requires customization. However, in some cases, it can be impractical because it might require the company to fundamentally change the way it runs its business. A common problem with customization is that it tends to be overdone because companies cannot distinguish between needs and wants. Excessive customization can be time consuming and also cause serious problems during software upgrades.

Inadequate preparation

ERP projects require extensive planning and preparation. Inadequate groundwork and preparation by the organization for migrating over to the new system can cause serious problems or even lead to outright failure. It can also prevent the new software from being used to its full potential.

Fear of failure

ERP failures, when announced, become headline news. The costs involved with write-offs can be staggering. Bad news travels fast and, therefore, it is no surprise that ERP failures have been well publicized within the IT and business communities. Therefore, whenever an ERP implementation is evaluated, it causes apprehension within company management. The decision to risk the business and one's own career, knowing that failure is a possibility, is not made easily or quickly.

Chapter 2
What is SAP

Background

The company

SAP AG, founded by five former IBM engineers in 1972, is based in Walldorf, Germany. SAP is an acronym for Systeme, Anwendungen, Produkte in der Datenverarbeitung, which means Systems, Applications and Products in Data Processing. SAP is the world's largest enterprise software company. It is also the world's third-largest independent software company, which is publicly traded on the Frankfurt Stock Exchange and the New York Stock Exchange. In fiscal year 2000, SAP's revenues were EUR 6.264 billion.

SAP employs over 27,800 people in more than 50 countries. It has a customer base exceeding 13,500 organizations, in 120 countries, with over 36,000 installations and 10 million users[4]. Businesses with annual revenues of less than $200 million represent more than one-third of SAP's worldwide installed base[5]. It also has over 10 million licensed users world-wide.

In addition to developing business applications software, SAP also provides extensive training and consulting services for implementing its software.

---

[4] SAP's web site, November 11, 2001
[5] informationweek.com, January 15, 2001, pg 8

Main product

SAP's main product is SAP™ R/3® software, which is available in 28 languages in 46 country-specific versions. SAP™ R/3® is a highly customizable, client/server, integrated software that was introduced in 1992. It is based on the ABAP/4® programming language. SAP™ R/3® is the successor to SAP™ R/2™, which operated on mainframes.

SAP introduced a scalable and Internet-ready architecture in 1996. With its introduction, SAP took the first step to position itself for capitalizing on the growing need for customer-centric, personalized and collaborative enterprise solutions. mySAP.com™ provides the architecture that enables an organization to bring together its customers, vendors, partners and employees in a collaborative, web-based, environment.

SAP customers

SAP has customers in all parts of the world. 36% of all global companies with revenues greater than $1 billion use SAP. This compares to only 8% for Oracle—its closest rival. More than half of the top 500 companies in the world use SAP.

SAP's customer list includes most of the U.S. Fortune 100 companies. All of the top ten US companies, by revenue and market capitalization, have used at least one kind of SAP software[6].

Initially, SAP was perceived to be a software company that only met the needs of large corporations—the billion dollar revenue companies. However, in the past few years, few billion dollar companies remained that had not implemented an ERP system. Therefore, due to the need to find new markets, SAP started to focus on the previously neglected mid- and small-sized companies. This was an interesting turn because SAP initially gained prominence as a software solution for small-sized organizations.

---

[6]Private communication; Waggener Edstrom Strategic Communications

Due to the recent explosive growth in e-Commerce and business-to-business (B2B) customer needs, and SAP's response to it as reflected by the SAP 4.6 upgrade, we can expect the type, size and number of SAP customers to change significantly in the coming years.

Comparing implementation benefits

Competitive implementation time

In 1999, The Meta Group released the results of a survey in which 63 international companies participated[7]. The objective was to compare the top seven ERP vendors. The survey revealed that their implementation periods ranged from a low of 18 months for SSA implementations to a high of 26 months for Oracle implementations. SAP's average implementation time was 20 months, which was better than the ERP vendor average of 23 months to get an ERP system up and running.

Financial benefits
Average benefits

Implementing SAP can result in an organization achieving significant financial benefits—which can accrue from a number of areas. The type, and magnitude, of the costs and benefits will be different for each implementation. According to The Meta Group survey referenced earlier, the average cost over a two year period was $10.6 million for the implementation and $2.1 million for maintenance.

Example of specific benefits

For an SAP implementation at a mid-cap company, with $400 million in annual revenues, the total financial benefits were estimated to be $43

---

[7] Information Week, May 24, 1999, pg 60

million over a two year period. The estimated breakdown of benefits in different areas, as a percentage of annual revenues, was as follows:
- Improved efficiency: 44%
- Revenue and profitability growth: 37%
- Increase customer loyalty: 14%
- Reduced risk due to obsolete systems: 5%

Characteristics of SAP™ R/3® software

Basic characteristics

SAP is a very powerful software with the following defining characteristics:

General
- Highly integrated and cross-functional software with tight integration across functions.
- Real time (the R in R/3 refers to real-time). Data update are done online and in real-time. For example, if a purchase order (PO) is issued (in the Materials Management module), the amount of the PO will be immediately reflected in the Finance module.

Business
- Comprehensive functionality is incorporated, which enables it to run complete businesses. It incorporates best industry practices and is suitable for a wide range of industries and organizations.
- Supports enterprise-wide business processes.

Flexibility
- Highly configurable. Can be customized according to a company's needs and requirements. Changes can be easy or difficult, depending on a number of factors such as the extent of customization.
- Can support enterprises with subsidiaries located at geographically scattered sites.
- Favored internationally due to its availability in 14 languages and ability to customize the software to currencies, tax laws, accounting procedures, import/export regulations, etc.

Technical
- Portable across databases, operating systems and front-ends.
- Characterized by minimum data redundancy, maximum data consistency, highly secure data handling and complex data structures.
- Complex package with technical implications that include software development, database administration, networking and production control.

Other features
- Same data is used across different functional modules.
- Single point of entry.
- Capitalizes on economy of scale; is very scalable.
- Easy-to use graphical user interface.

Best business practices

SAP includes more than 1,000 predefined processes that represent best business practices. These encompass a wide range of functional requirements. More of these are being added as part of SAP's effort to help its customers meet the demanding needs of a rapidly changing business environment in these fast-paced times.

Industry-specific functionality

A number of industries are supported by SAP through solutions and functionality that addresses their unique requirements. The 21 industry solutions that SAP can deliver include:

- Aerospace and defense
- Automotive
- Banking
- Chemicals
- Consumer products
- Engineering and construction
- Financial service provider
- Health care
- Higher education and research
- High technology
- Insurance
- Media
- Mill products
- Mining
- Oil and gas
- Pharmaceuticals
- Public sector
- Retail
- Service providers
- Telecommunications
- Utilities

For each of these industries, SAP has created a solution that reflects their specific business process requirements including web-enabled processes. These solutions incorporate best business practices. Additionally, SAP partners have created many solutions that are industry-specific. At the end of the year 2000, there were 29 industry solutions in use or development[8].

Customization
Need for customization

ERP packages, and SAP in particular, are fairly complicated. This is the result of trying to achieve functionality that is all-encompassing and capable of meeting the varied needs of tens of thousands of customers. Typically, a customer selects an ERP package that meets most of the organization's business requirements. However, in order to run all parts of the business, the generic software package needs to be tailored so that it can meet the customer's specific needs and requirements. For example, if a functionality gap is identified during analysis, software customization becomes imperative if the option of modifying the business practice is discarded.

While it is understandable that SAP needs to be modified to meet the business requirements of a company, the problem lies in over-customization. This occurs when an attempt is made to make SAP look and feel like the legacy system(s) being discarded.

How customization is done

A number of tools and utilities are available for customizing SAP according to the specific needs of the customer. Customization is typically done by consultants, project team members and IT personnel.

There are basically two methods for SAP customization required to achieve the needed functionality. These are:

---

[8]informationweek.com, January 15, 2001, pg 8

- Configuration changes: these involve table entries which are configurable
- ABAP/4® programming: this involves modifying existing programs within the SAP™ R/3® software or writing completely new programs which are incorporated into the main software

Complexity of customization

Some SAP customization is relatively simple. However, it can be fairly complex even for experienced consultants, especially during the initial implementation, to tailor the software according to a customer's specific needs. While ERP vendors have made a significant effort to simplify this process, it still requires a significant amount of time and effort.

Problem in customizing

The amount, and type, of customization that can be done by a customer is extensive. It is possible to modify the SAP source code (or logic), or add tables and columns, if the functionality to be supported requires it. However, besides being expensive, extensive customization creates a problem whenever the software is upgraded. Each upgrade and new software release, which can occur a few times every year, can become a maintenance and testing nightmare if major customization has been performed.

Support provided by SAP

TeamSAP™ approach

The TeamSAP™ approach combines SAP resources, including personnel and technology, with that of its more than 1,000 partners. These partners are classified into eight categories:

- ❏ Software partners
- ❏ Service partners
- ❏ Technology partners
- ❏ Support partners
- ❏ Hosting partners
- ❏ Channel partners
- ❏ Content partners
- ❏ Education partners

The TeamSAP™ approach enables fast, customer-specific, and efficient implementation for SAP clients. With over 45,000 consultants trained in SAP™ R/3® software, there is a vast pool of resources available to draw upon for any SAP implementation.

Service and support

SAP does not limit its support to evaluation and implementation of its software. Besides aiming for continuous business improvement, it also provides 24x7 service and support to its customers.

Training

SAP provides training in a number of formats including conventional, classroom-based, training and remote real-time Internet training. It offers more than 200 courses, taught by more than 150 instructors, at 85 training centers across the world. SAP also has a program that works with colleges and universities at different locations.

Chapter 3
Functionality and architecture

Functional architecture

SAP modules

SAP™ R/3® software consists of the following functional modules:
1. Asset Management (AM)
2. Financials (FI)
3. Controlling (CO)
4. Human Resources (HR)
5. Plant Maintenance (PM)
6. Production Planning (PP)
7. Project System (PS)
8. Quality Management (QM)
9. Sales and Distribution (SD)
10. Materials Management (MM)
11. Service Management (SM)
12. Industry Specific Solutions (IS)
13. Business Workflow (WF)
14. Basis (includes ABAP/4® programming language) (BC)

Each of these modules has a number of sub-modules. For example, the Financials (FI) module contains sub-modules for Financial Accounting, Controlling, Investment Management, Treasury Cash Management, Enterprise controlling and Real Estate.

Integration between modules

The software that SAP provides to its customers includes all the modules. However, each customer retains the choice of selecting the modules that will be implemented. These modules are tightly integrated and, in many cases, specific functionality can be accessed through different modules. For example, a vendor's data can be accessed from both the Financials and Materials Management modules.

Functionality by module

The following is a list of the most important functions supported by each module:

Financial & Asset Accounting
- General ledger
- Accounts receivable
- Accounts payable
- Asset accounting
- Leased assets
- Special purpose ledger
- Legacy consolidations
- Financial accounting information system

Controlling
- ❏ Overhead cost controlling
- ❏ Product cost controlling
- ❏ Profitability analysis
- ❏ Activity based costing
- ❏ Internal orders

Investment Management
- ❏ Investment plans (budgets)
- ❏ Investments (orders and projects)
- ❏ Automatic settlement of fixed assets
- ❏ Depreciation forecast

Treasury
- ❏ Cash management
- ❏ Treasury management
- ❏ Market risk management
- ❏ Funds management

Enterprise Controlling
- ❏ Business planning and budgeting
- ❏ Consolidations
- ❏ Profit center accounting
- ❏ Intercompany transactions
- ❏ Executive information system

Real Estate
- Rental administration and settlement
- Controlling, position valuation and information management

Human Resources
- Personnel administration
    - Payroll
    - Benefits administration
    - Recruitment
    - Time management
    - Travel management
    - Compensation management
- Personnel planning and development
    - Organization management
    - Training and events management

Plant Maintenance
- Preventive maintenance
- Service management
- Maintenance projects
- Maintenance notifications
- Maintenance orders
- Equipment and technical objects
- Plant maintenance information system

Production Planning
- ❏ Sales and operations planning
- ❏ Master production scheduling
- ❏ Materials requirements planning
- ❏ Capacity requirements planning
- ❏ KANBAN
- ❏ Repetitive manufacturing
- ❏ Make-to-stock
- ❏ Production orders
- ❏ Product cost planning
- ❏ Assembly orders
- ❏ Production planning for process industries
- ❏ Shop floor control
- ❏ Work centers
- ❏ Routings
- ❏ Bill of materials
- ❏ Production planning and control information systems

Project System
- ❏ Operational structures - work breakdown structure
- ❏ Networks and resources
- ❏ Project execution and integration
- ❏ Project evaluation (project information system)
- ❏ Budget management
- ❏ Cost and revenue planning

Quality Management
- Quality planning
- Quality inspections
- Quality control
- Notifications
- Test equipment management
- Quality management information system
- Inspection processing

Sales and Distribution
- Quotations
- Sales order management
- Pricing
- Shipping
- Billing
- Foreign trade
- Sales information system
- Availability check and requirements
- Computer aided sales

Materials Management
- Procurement
- Inventory management
- Materials planning
- Vendor evaluation
- Invoice verification
- Warehouse management
- Logistics information system
- Consumption-based planning

Service Management
- ❏ Services such as warranty, maintenance and repair work
- ❏ Service agreements
- ❏ Service notifications
- ❏ Service orders

Business Processes
- ❏ Business workflow
- ❏ Office system

Basis Components
- ❏ ABAP/4® development workbench
- ❏ Computing center management system
- ❏ Multiple system utilities
- ❏ User management and authorization concept
- ❏ Transport and correction system
- ❏ Client management
- ❏ Data archiving
- ❏ Printer management and output control

Physical architecture

Three-tier client/server architecture

The SAP™ R/3® system is based on the distributed client/server architecture. It includes three components: database layer, application layer and presentation layer. Physically, the system consists of database servers, application servers and clients (user desktops) connected through a network. In the three-tier client/server architecture, a distinct separation exists between the different layers as described in the following sections.

Database layer

The database layer consists of a database server where the data is stored. It provides the central storage and management of the company's working data, which includes master data and transaction data. It also holds the metadata, which is maintained in the repository, that describes the database structure. Due to the central storage of data, SAP is able to maintain data consistency and seamless integration between modules. The database server software manages and controls various functions such as database management and batch processing.

SAP, designed as an open system, uses relational databases for data storage. It supports the major relational database management systems (RDBMS) from vendors including Oracle, Informix, IBM and Microsoft. SAP™ R/3® uses structured query language (SQL) for defining and manipulating data. It also supports proprietary SQL enhancements.

Application layer

The application layer consists of an application server where the business logic/rules reside and application logic is processed. The function of application servers is to prepare and process incoming data. For example, a user request to read or write data is processed by the application server before being sent to the database server. Custom ABAP™ applications are processed by the application server. SAP administrative functions are also managed at this layer.

Presentation layer

The presentation layer facilitates interaction between the user and the computer. This layer includes the graphical user interface (GUI), which displays the R/3™ window. The presentation layer typically resides on the user's desktop. The interaction process involves the GUI receiving a user request, which it passes on to the application server for further processing.

Advantages of a decentralized system

There are many advantages of using a decentralized architecture for an ERP system like SAP. These include:

> Scalability

SAP supports an unlimited number of users as well as database and application servers in a variety of hardware configurations. This flexibility enables a company to start on a relatively small-scale. Later on, when expansion becomes necessary, additional database or application servers can be added to the network. For example, if the number of users increases, more clients (PCs) can be added. If the quantity of data to be processed increases significantly, more database servers can be added without requiring an overall system upgrade. This scalability advantage at any level (database, application or presentation), makes SAP an attractive option for different types of organizations—both large and small.

> Open system

Plug and play is encouraged by this system. Hardware/peripherals from different vendors can be used, which can lead to more competition and lower costs.

> Workload distribution

It is easier for an administrator to distribute the load on various servers. For example, the primary users of a specific module, such as Finance, can be routed to a particular server for load balancing.

> Response time

It is possible to achieve near instant response times, despite simultaneous usage by hundreds of users, with a decentralized architecture.

➢ Higher availability to users

Compared to mainframes, higher system availability is possible for users because they need not logoff to run batch jobs, which can be processed in the background.

➢ Ease of use

Decentralized systems such as SAP support a PC-based user-friendly interface. They are easier to interact with compared to mainframe dumb terminals.

Platforms supported

SAP is a software that can run on many operating systems including Unix (for which it was originally designed), Windows NT, Windows 2000, AS/400 and Linux. In January 2000, SAP shipped its 10,000th installation of SAP solutions on Windows NT. In 1999, more than 60% of all new installations of SAP solutions were on Windows, a total of more than 2,5000 installations worldwide[9].

SAP also supports a number of relational databases including Oracle, Informix, IBM DB2, Microsoft's SQL Server and SAP DB. For presentation, SAP supports Java, Web browser, MS Windows, OSF/Motif and OS/2 Presentation Manager.

Understanding SAP's environment

The following sections describe the primary architectural elements of the SAP system and its organization structure. For those who need to implement SAP, familiarity with the organizational structure is a basic requirement because it is the foundation upon which the system is ultimately configured and built.

---

[9]IntelligentERP, October 20, 2000, pg 6

Structural elements
Instance

A single installation of the SAP source code/modules is called an "Instance." Each version of the SAP™ R/3® software, such as 3.0 and 4.0, requires a separate system. There is no integration of data or functionality between systems as delivered.

In a typical SAP system, the various functional requirements are usually achieved by setting up the following instances:

- Development instance

  In this box, developers and configurators perform their development work. Configuration, programs, SAP Scripts, forms, reports, etc., are developed and initially tested here. After testing has been completed, these objects are moved to a more formal testing environment—the testing instance.

- Testing instance

  This is the quality assurance (QA) box where rigorous testing, typically based on an established methodology, is performed. After completion of QA testing, objects are moved to the production instance.

- Production instance

  This is the production system where the company's business is run. It is the place where the users perform their day-to-day work.

- Training instance

  In this box, users are trained to use SAP before being authorized to work in the production instance.

Client

An instance can be further organized and sub-divided into different sections, called clients. For example, a typical development instance architecture will include separate clients for:

- Developers (Client 100)
- Configurators (Client 200)
- Data migration and load testing (Client 300)

The following is a list of some important client characteristics:
- A physical database, or an instance, may have multiple SAP clients
- Different clients have separate, unrelated, data
- Data of one client may not be accessed by another client
- Full functional and data integration occurs within a client
- Minimal integration exists between clients
- Financial consolidations across clients are possible
- Single logical database; in a system, all clients reside within the same database

Organizational structure
Client

A client is the basic and highest organizational unit within SAP. It represents an organization or a logical grouping of multiple companies. It is a self-contained, commercially and organizationally independent, unit. A client has its own separate data environment including customization, master data, transaction data, user master records and set of tables.

An organizational structure client, which represents a corporate hierarchy, should not be confused with the client(s) associated with an instance, which is a unit of the SAP physical architecture.

Company code

A company code, which is the smallest unit displaying a complete external accounting unit, is the basic organizational unit in the SAP accounting system. It is at the company code level that the profit and loss statement is generated. It is possible for a single or several company codes to exist for a single client.

Chapter 4
Impact of SAP implementations

Analyzing failures

High profile failures

There have been many high profile ERP and SAP implementation failures in recent years. In 1999, Hershey Foods suffered a major problem in its $112 million SAP™ R/3® system. Problems included lost orders, missed shipments and disgruntled customers. For the third-quarter, revenues were down $151 million from 1998[10].

While most problems are ultimately resolved, some companies have chosen to scrap problem SAP implementations, in the past few years, despite having spent tens of millions of dollars. For example, Unisource Worldwide, Inc, a $7 billion distributor of paper products, wrote off $168 million in costs related to an SAP implementation[11]. Even on a smaller scale, the losses can be very painful, such as the $10.7 million write-off by Entex Information Services—a $2.5 billion systems integration and outsourcing company[12].

---

[10] CIO, February 15, 2000, pg 71
[11] www.techweb.com April 22, 1998
[12] Information Week, March 8, 1999, pg 24

Types of SAP project failures

There are literally thousands of SAP projects that have been quite successful. However, a large number of SAP projects have also been characterized by:

- ❏ Delays: implementation took much longer than expected
- ❏ Cost overruns: cost to implement was much greater than anticipated
- ❏ Cancellations: after spending years and millions of dollars

Additionally, despite making huge investments in SAP™ R/3® software, many companies have found that their business performance did not improve as expected. In such cases, with few exceptions, the software has been blamed. However, professionals experienced in implementing SAP know that despite some drawbacks associated with the software, there are many other failure causes that cannot be attributed to the software itself. These causes are explained in the following sections.

Explaining failures

The following are some of the common reasons, among companies that have been through a less-than-fully successful SAP implementation, for poor results.

Wrong software selection

When anticipated results do not materialize, ERP software vendors are usually blamed. Are ERP vendors that sold the software the real culprits because business performance did not improve or the implementation was flawed? The fact is that the blame is often misplaced. Certainly, it can be argued that a particular ERP system's logic is sometimes illogical, lacks the required functionality, performs poorly, and so on. However, accountability for ERP software selection needs to be shared by internal staff and external consultants who are involved in the evaluation process.

In the final analysis, the ultimate responsibility for analyzing and selecting an ERP package resides with the company. If it selects SAP, and later finds out that the choice was wrong because it could not support critical business functionality, then the company should not blame SAP.

Inadequate planning

Selecting and implementing a new ERP system, and the process changes that go with it, is unquestionably a complex undertaking. Regardless of size and perceived resources, an SAP implementation should be approached with a great deal of careful planning. Many failures can be attributed to pre-implementation preparation activities that were done poorly, if at all.

Inadequate organization structure

An organized approach, backed by a well-structured project organization, is a basic requirement for an SAP implementation. In many cases, where an ERP implementation failed to deliver, failure can be attributed to management that did not adequately structure the organization—either before implementation or after go-live.

Lack of understanding

There is a widespread lack of understanding of the unique nature and elements that are involved in an SAP project. This ignorance can extend to all levels of the project hierarchy as well as business/corporate management.

Not appreciating implementation complexity

SAP™ R/3® software cannot be implemented with the approach used to implement a simple, stand-alone, business software. There are too many factors that come into play with SAP implementations. For example, every company and business is unique. Even within the same industry, no two companies operate in exactly the same way. Corporate cultures vary and the level of commitment to a project can vary. Also, the mix of legacy systems and applications in operation at every organization is different. Therefore, the integration effort required, and the complexity of customization, varies at each site. Another unique factor is that all the existing legacy systems need simultaneous replacement in a risky operation.

The availability of skills influences the level of complexity that can be handled. This includes the skill level and:

- ❏ dedication of project personnel drawn from the company's ranks
- ❏ approach of the integrators and implementation consultants, which varies considerably

All these factors, along with a number of others, combine to make SAP a very complex implementation project.

Unable to understand implementation risks

All software projects, and SAP projects in particular, are exposed to many risks. One of the critical elements required to prevent an SAP project failure is understanding the risks involved. Failure to understand implementation risks can cause an organization to approach the project in a casual way, which can increase the failure risk considerably.

Being over ambitious

SAP is loaded with features. Therefore, it is not surprising that there is a tendency to be over ambitious and try to implement every feature possible. Consequently, the implementation scope is increased—intentionally as well as unintentionally. Trying to get too much done in too short a period can be very risky. A conservative approach, which works very well, is to get SAP up and running with the minimum functionality required to make the business run. Additional features and enhancements are added during subsequent phases.

Operating strategy did not drive business process design and deployment

Many manufacturers fail to realize that extensive supply chain improvement requires that management redefine the business in terms of strategic opportunities. The SAP objective is to implement business processes that support the company's strategic objectives. Therefore, business process design and deployment should be driven by the operating strategy which, in many cases, does not happen.

Rush to completion

Many of the recent failures, especially during 1999, have been attributed to looming Y2K deadlines. These may have caused implementation teams to rush what, normally, they would have done more gradually. Some ERP issues have been blamed on vendors, including SAP, prematurely rushing out new products and releases. This can be attributed to stiff competition in the supply chain, e-Commerce, and customer relationship management arenas.

Not prepared to accept the new system

For an SAP project to be successfully implemented, an organization and its employees need to be prepared. Preparation, implementation and readiness to accept change are very important ingredients for success. For companies that were not prepared to change the way in which they operated in the past, failure came their way quite easily.

What SAP does to an organization

Re-engineering

SAP is a re-engineering driver. It forces companies to review all their existing business processes. The result is that many of SAP's processes, which represent best business practices, are selected to replace the existing ones that, in many cases, are quite obsolete.

Impacts corporate culture

SAP can have a visible impact on corporate culture. It can open up new and better ways of doing business. For example, at one highly bureaucratic company, it led to reducing the approval hierarchy for requisitions from an average of 10 to only 4 people. It kills the philosophy that causes people to resist change by using the excuse "because we have always been doing it this way." It forces people to think out of the box.

Changes competitive landscape

With improved processes, greater agility, quicker response to customer needs, and improved vendor relationship, a company using SAP is better prepared to mount a serious challenge to its competitors or, if it is the leader, maintain its competitive lead.

Creates inter-dependency

The integrated nature of the software makes employees working in different functional groups more aware of how the other functional groups operate. It creates an appreciation of the problems and issues that the other functional groups are exposed to. For example, other groups quickly know it when a mistake is made in one functional area (such as finance) because it immediately impacts other areas (such as purchasing or sales) due to the integrated nature of the software. Hence, the tendency to work in functional silos decreases considerably.

Shifts balance of power

SAP empowers business users. They take over the system and IT is relegated to a secondary role. Business users can make decisions and implement changes, such as process and configuration changes, on their own without requiring IT approval or help. While IT is a partner, it is the business users who are in the driver's seat. After implementation, low level managers and employees discover that they have access to a tremendous amount of data and reports regarding the company, and its operations, that they never had previously. This makes employees feel empowered.

Simplifies platform

With the retirement of a number of legacy systems and applications, which typically operate on different types of platforms, the total number and variety of systems that an organization needs to maintain decreases dramatically. Also, the retiring outdated systems are replaced by a system that better reflects current technology and is easier to maintain.

Impacts costs/profitability

It is simpler and cheaper to maintain fewer systems and applications. Therefore, replacing a number of legacy systems with an SAP system can translate into lower costs and, consequently, profitability.

Impacts employees

Human nature is such that any change can cause anxiety. Therefore, it is no surprise that an SAP implementation introduces fear and stress among employees. The fear is that with the introduction of the new software, existing skill sets will become obsolete. That translates into an inability to perform one's job after the new software is implemented. Employees also fear that existing jobs may be eliminated and/or redefined. All this forces employees to deal with change. However, the net result is that employees are forced to upgrade their skills, which is positive for them in the long run.

Impacts work environment

The work environment changes in many ways. Users feel empowered because they have increased information access and the ability to make changes to a powerful system. They are able to move out of their silos and observe what happens elsewhere. For example, a buyer is able to trace the history of a transaction that he initiated, such as creating a purchase order, all the way to the end of the process through the other modules. This would include access to all intermediate transactions such as Accounts Payable and Goods Receipt. Therefore, employees end up having a better understanding of other areas outside their functional silos.

SAP supports a paperless mode operation, which changes the way users meet their reporting needs. The philosophy is that since everything is available online, many of the existing hardcopy reports should no longer be generated. Also, due to the validity checks built in, and since a single common database is used by all users, confidence in the data and results increases.

It should be no surprise that there are also some negatives. Due to easy information access, security concerns increase. For example, a lot of problems can be created if salary information is leaked or other confidential information is compromised. Also, reports available in the new SAP system may not be comparable to the customized reports previously available to the users.

Provides flexibility

Most of the required changes, over time, can be accommodated by configuration changes—rather than programming. This flexibility is a big plus. Business users can implement these changes and, consequently, their dependence on IT is decreased.

Influences development

SAP employs over 6,000 software developers worldwide[13]. It periodically brings out new releases and features, based on the input of thousands of its customers. Therefore, it effectively becomes the application developer for those who have implemented SAP. Consequently, organizations that use SAP can expect to have an application that will not be outdated due to lack of upgrades or functionality improvements. They will always have access to a very current system. Therefore, their need for internal development will decrease significantly.

---

[13]informationweek.com, February 19, 2001, pg 136

Chapter 5
Implementation methodologies

How SAP projects are implemented

Basic essentials
The basic steps required to implement SAP are the following:
- Determine that the company is ready for implementation: an organization needs to be ready for change and its management has to be fully behind the project.
- Develop an implementation plan: without it, there will either be a slow and grinding project or a disaster.
- Develop the budget: this is a very critical factor that drives many elements including scope and schedule; depending on the methodology (big bang versus phased implementation and type of cost structure (such as fixed cost project), the overall implementation cost and budget can vary considerably.
- Select the implementation partners: this determines the quality and level of external skills and experience that will be available for the project.

Implementation roadmap
The essential steps required to implement SAP are the following:

1. Modeling:
   This involves defining the business processes that the organization desires to be in place after implementation. These are known as the "to-be" business processes.
2. Mapping:
   This step involves comparing the business processes, identified in step 1, to the SAP processes. This mapping identifies which SAP processes and functionality meet the future requirements of the company. These processes are selected for implementation.
3. Gap analysis:
   The shortcomings or gaps, between the requirements of the modeled processes and what SAP can provide, are identified.
4. Scoping:
   In this stage, after the identification of what can (or cannot) be implemented in SAP has been completed, the project scope is finalized.
5. Customizing:
   The SAP™ R/3® software is customized so that it can meet the business and functional requirements of the company. This is done through the Implementation Guide for R/3 Customizing (IMG).
6. Testing:
   The configured system is subjected to extensive testing to ensure that the software works as required.

Big versus small approach

There are two implementation approaches that are generally followed for SAP projects. These are:

Big bang approach

In this approach, a full-blown SAP system is implemented. All the modules required by the company are configured and implemented. All legacy systems that can be replaced by SAP are targeted for retirement. All divisions and/or subsidiaries of the company are included in the single-phase project. This approach is very time consuming, heavy on resources and costs, and very risky as well.

Phased approach

In this approach, which is modest in nature, a step-by-step implementation is undertaken. The overall project is implemented in a number of phases. The objective is to avoid risk and work on smaller, and more manageable, projects. A number of options exist within the phased approach method. The following are some of the available options:

- Option 1:
  - phase 1: only Finance and Logistics for all divisions
  - phase 2: remaining modules for all divisions
- Option 2:
  - phase 1: all modules for one division
  - phase 2: all modules for remaining divisions
- Option 3:
  - phase 1: only Finance and Logistics for one division
  - phase 2: remaining modules for the first division
  - phase 3: all modules for other divisions

Implementation methodologies

Conventional methodology

There are two methodologies used to implement SAP projects: Conventional and ASAP^{TM}. The conventional methodology, better known as the SAP Procedure Model, was initially widely used to implement SAP. In the past few years, it has been overshadowed by the rapid ASAP^{TM} methodology. However, it is still the preferred methodology for implementing SAP at very large companies, especially for those with revenues over a billion dollars.

The SAP Procedure Model implementation can be divided into four major phases:
- Organization and conceptual design
- Detailed design and system setup
- Go-live preparations
- Productive operations

This methodology requires that a very detailed analysis of the existing systems, current functionality, and business processes be conducted. A significant amount of time is spent on matching "as-is" and "to-be" systems. Decision-making is very slow as it is based on consensus, which takes time to achieve.

A drawback of the Procedure Model is that even though it did not dictate it, too many implementations tried to mirror existing systems within SAP. Another negative of this methodology is that it uses a company's existing processes, instead of the SAP processes, as the starting point for the mapping process. Therefore, it has been usual for Procedure Model-based projects to have the following results:
- Lengthy implementation periods
- Scope continued to increase as analysis dragged on

ASAP™ methodology

In an effort to speed up SAP projects and keep costs under control, SAP introduced the ASAP™ methodology, which has been quite successful to-date. While a conventional project can typically take a couple of years, or even more in many cases, an ASAP™ project can be easily implemented within a year. With the ASAP™ methodology, an implementation period as short as five months has been achieved. This methodology is explained in-depth in the following sections and chapters.

Comparing conventional and ASAP™ methodologies

As with any methodology, there are pros and cons associated with both the SAP methodologies. For some implementations, especially those that require major re-engineering, the conventional methodology is the better choice. However, as the benefits listed in the following table show, the ASAP™ methodology is the clear overall winner.

		ASAP™ versus Conventional methodology	
		ASAP™	Conventional
1.	Time frame	Fast implementation	Slow implementation
2.	Approach	Rushed without in-depth analysis	Based on extensive analysis and consensus
3.	Re-engineering	More due to implementation of new SAP supported processes	Less because tendency is to mirror existing processes
4.	Features/functionality	Vanilla	Custom
5.	Implementation	Very focused and narrow	Comprehensive
6.	Configuration	Primarily done by consultants	Significant employee participation
7.	Upgrades	Less testing required as minimal code changes are implemented	More testing required due to extensive code modifications
8.	Cost	Low	High
9.	Documentation	Minimal	Extensive
10.	ABAP™ development	Minimal due to vanilla implementation	Extensive due to excessive custom requirements
11.	Number of consultants	Relatively few are required	Large team of experts is required
12.	Employee turnover	Low due to less knowledge gained during implementation	High as extensive knowledge gained can be leveraged for a better job
13.	Knowledge transfer for employees	Low since project is rushed and consultants allocate insufficient time	High since features are configured gradually with employee participation

Chapter 6
ASAP™ methodology

Background and overview

Need for ASAP™

ERP packages, especially SAP, encompass a broad range of functionality. During a typical project, only some of this functionality can be implemented. Since the specific needs and requirements of implementing companies can vary significantly, the software needs to be customized to meet their individual requirements. Therefore, a satisfactory implementation that can address these issues, as well as others, can take a fairly long time that can be costly and fraught with risks.

With the conventional SAP implementation methodology, it was very difficult to configure flexibly and quickly. This conflicted with the requirements of mid-sized companies who demanded rapid implementation that could be measured in months instead of years. Therefore, with time being of the essence and a fast implementation being a difficult objective to achieve, it became apparent that a different implementation approach was required.

SAP's realization that it needed to be more responsive to the needs of its customers led to the introduction of the AcceleratedSAP™ (ASAP) rapid implementation methodology in 1996. ASAP™ initially targeted mid-sized customers with revenues in the $200 million to $2.5 billion range.

A point to note is that in a shift from the past, ASAP™ reflected a change from focusing on tools to an emphasis on methodology. It is a methodology that supports project management, team members, business process consultants, external consultants, as well as technical areas.

What ASAP™ can do

ASAP™ has been designed with the objective of standardizing and streamlining SAP implementation. The following is a list of ASAP™ characteristics:

- Optimizes time, quality and resources
- Leverages best business practices
- Delivers a process oriented project map (ASAP™ roadmap) that provides step-by-step directions
- Determines implementation cost and schedule; cuts implementation cost and time
- Provides process, tools, training and service
- Provides detailed help through various implementation phases
- Answers questions about implementation cost and time, how to ensure quality, tools to use, and resources required
- Provides checklists, questionnaires and technical guides
- Supports continuous improvement

How ASAP™ is implemented

Organizations implementing SAP typically do not have the in-house expertise required to implement the complex software. Therefore, it is usual for such companies to partner with an external organization, such as one of the Big 5 consulting companies or a smaller integrator, to implement their SAP project.

SAP recommends that its clients team up with an ASAP™ partner when they implement an SAP project. A company obtains ASAP™ partner certification if at least 70% of its consultants have completed ASAP™ training and it has fully adopted the ASAP methodology.

ASAP™ implementation costs

No two SAP implementations are identical because there are too many variables involved. Variables include the company size, number of divisions/subsidiaries, number of systems, overall scope, approach, company culture, experience of partners, etc. Therefore, it is difficult to generalize the cost of implementing SAP at an organization.

A few studies have been conducted that provide some guidelines regarding the magnitude of the costs involved in implementing SAP. One such study by the Aberdeen Group, in June 1998, was based on three SAP installations using the ASAP™ methodology. This study determined that implementation costs at these sites could be broken down as follows:

- Consulting fees: 36%
- In-house labor: 21%
- Software license fees: 20%
- Training fees: 6%
- Hardware costs: 17%

When ASAP™ is not an appropriate choice

The ASAP™ methodology is not appropriate for all types of SAP implementations. It is ideally suited for enterprises that do not have extensive modification requirements or require re-engineering. For such companies, other methodologies are more appropriate.

ASAP™ is the methodology of choice when rapid deployment is highly stressed. However, when there is more emphasis on process improvement than on rapid deployment, which occurs when enterprises require significant process and operational improvements or re-engineering, the conventional implementation methodology is a more appropriate choice.

Current ASAP™ status

ASAP™ is now established as the SAP standard implementation methodology. Since its introduction, ASAP™ has been used in more than 1,000 projects worldwide. A very large pool of experts, comprising more than 18,000 SAP and partner consultants, has been trained in this methodology. Many of SAP's implementation partners are either using ASAP™ as their standard methodology or have incorporated it into their own methodologies.

ASAP™ components and tools

Where can they be used

SAP has provided a number of components, tools and accelerators for supporting ASAP™ implementations. ASAP™ components, which can be used in any type of SAP project, include forms, questionnaires and guides. Many ASAP™ partners use ASAP methodology components in conjunction with their own implementation methodologies and practices.

ASAP™ tools and accelerators, which can be used to streamline and improve implementations, are described in the following sections. While these tools were developed for ASAP™ implementations, most of them can also be used during SAP implementations based on the conventional methodology. Various ASAP™ components, functions and organizational structures can be tailored, or deactivated, to suit individual requirements.

R/3™ Reference Model

This visual tool represents the SAP™ R/3® system using graphical models. It depicts, among other aspects, business processes along with any variants, data, as well as organizational structures. The R/3™ reference model, which helps in seeing the bigger picture, can be accessed through the Business Navigator. This tool links the process models to SAP transactions.

Toolkit

The Toolkit includes all the ASAP™ tools such as the Business Engineer, Project Estimator and Implementation Assistant. Each of these tools serves a specific purpose. A number of the Toolkit tools are described in the following sections.

Business Engineer

The R/3™ Business Engineer (BE) is a set of configuration and implementation tools for modeling, configuration, implementation, continuous improvement and documentation. ASAP™ utilizes the Business Engineer's powerful capabilities for configuring the system. The Business Engineer and the tools contained within it:

- Provide a toolkit of specific business processes for expediting implementation
- Incorporate over 1,000 business processes and more than 170 core business objects
- Incorporate best business practices
- Simplify configuration
- Support custom configuration
- Allow graphical methods for viewing, navigation and configuration
- Efficiently expedite R/3™ configuration
- Support changes and system improvements required due to business changes
- Enable easy modification of the corporate structure
- Can adapt existing configuration to new requirements/changes

Together, ASAP™ and the Business Engineer can help to:
- Use industry specific business processes and templates
- Determine which R/3™ processes are most suitable for the company
- Implement new processes or restructure existing ones
- Optimize business processes through the use of proven scenarios and processes both during, and after, implementation
- Provide structured planning and pre-configuration
- Configure according to each individual requirement
- Manage time, cost and quality
- Reduce implementation time
- Attain a faster return on investment

The Business Engineer can be used by a broad audience including consultants, business professionals and experts, as well as all types of companies—large, medium and small. It supports HTML based documentation, new platforms, as well as modeling tools and software provided by independent vendors.

Project Estimator

This is a pre-sales tool that is used to estimate the resources, time and cost required to implement SAP at a particular site. The Project Estimator relies on a series of pre-defined interview questions that are posed to the company's senior executives, business and technical managers, as well as project team members. The purpose is to gather information needed to assess:
- Expectations
- Company expertise: strengths and weaknesses
- Degree of complexity of business processes
- Project scope
- Deployment time desired
- SAP team expertise
- Risk factors

The information gathered is used to create a high level estimate. It is also used to create the scope document and project plan.

Implementation Assistant

The Implementation Assistant serves as a navigation tool for the ASAP™ Implementation Roadmap, described in a later section, which provides guidance during various implementation phases. It consists of many tools and elements, such as the:

- ASAP™ Roadmap: which consists of five phases
- Project Plan: which contains the budget, resource and work plans
- Knowledge Corner: which is a warehouse of information encompassing configuration, technical tools, customizing wizards, etc.

The Implementation Assistant has the following features:

- Covers the five ASAP™ implementation phases down to the task level
- Includes a description for each Roadmap task
- Provides guidance through every Roadmap task
- Indicates which tasks are to be performed, who needs to be designated to do it, and how long it should take to finish
- Includes a detailed "how-to" for each Roadmap task; shows how to perform specific tasks, complete checklists, check with technical guidelines, etc.
- Links documents accessed through the Roadmap
- Includes specific examples, templates, forms and checklists
- Provides hyperlinks from tasks to tools, templates and documents
- Contains extensive testing guide that can help configure associated business processes
- Provides capability to drill down into work packages, activities and tasks from the Roadmap's five phases

Question and Answer Database

This is a tool that is used to gather requirements for:
- Business processes
- Conversions
- Reports
- Interfaces
- Enhancements
- Authorizations

The questions and answers are stored in a database, which serves as a useful repository for this information. The business requirements generated through the Question and Answer database are incorporated in the Business Blueprint document.

Issues Database

This tool is used to document issues and concerns that arise during project implementation. A common and central location ensures that all identified issues receive high visibility. It also ensures easier assignment, monitoring and updating of the recorded issues.

ASAP™ Roadmap

This ASAP™ component defines a systematic approach and methodology that incorporates a project plan for an SAP implementation. For various project activities, it describes:
- What is to be done
- Why it is needed
- How it is to be performed
- Who should implement it

The Roadmap is a step-by-step guide that is divided into five phases. These are:

- Phase 1: Project Preparation
- Phase 2: Business Blueprint
- Phase 3: Realization (includes Simulation and Validation)
- Phase 4: Final Preparation
- Phase 5: Go-Live and Support

The implementation time required for each phase depends on the total project implementation time that, typically, ranges between 6 and 18 months for ASAP™ projects. For example, at a mid-cap company project, for which the total implementation time was one year, the approximate time spent on each phase was as follows:

- Project Preparation: 1 month
- Business Blueprint: 2 months
- Realization: 6 months: (2 months for Simulation + 4 months for Validation)
- Final Preparation: 3 months

In another project at a 2 billion dollar company, which lasted 18 months, the breakdown was as follows:

- Project Preparation: 1 month
- Business Blueprint: 5 months
- Realization: 9 months (4 months for Simulation + 5 months for Validation)
- Final Preparation: 3 months

Accelerators

ASAP™ uses components called accelerators that include examples, checklists, templates, etc. Depending on a project's requirements, an accelerator can be used in conjunction with other tools. Accelerators can be used in any type of implementation, even if all ASAP™ components are not used in that implementation.

An accelerator can be used by an implementation partner, even when a different approach and methodology is being followed, to meet implementation objectives. These objectives, which are usually in sync with those of an ASAP™ project, can include speedier implementation, lower cost, efficient resource utilization, quality improvement, etc.

Project Quality Check

A project quality review is conducted during the important phases of an implementation. The objective of this review is to assess the various areas (including technical, business and management), gauge progress made, review deliverables and assess risks.

EarlyWatch™

This is a preventive service offered by SAP. It allows SAP experts to proactively analyze the system before going live. Based on its findings, SAP makes recommendations for optimizing applications and performance so that potential production problems can be avoided. This helps ensure that when the system goes live, most parameters are well tuned and the system is optimized.

EarlyWatch™ is just one of the many services and support that SAP can provide. Others include the Online Service System (OSS), Concept Check and Going Live check. Each of these tools is used for quality assurance.

Concept Check Tool

This tool is used to investigate the technical aspects of the project by performing quality checks. These checks are used to:

- Verify that the application has been correctly configured
- Provide data for the Going Live check that is performed at the end of the project
- Provide warning of potential performance issues due to data volume and configuration conflicts

Chapter 7
Phase 1 - Project Preparation

There are many factors that can lead to the success or failure of an ASAP™ or any other type of software project. One of the critical factors, especially for SAP projects, is organizational readiness and project preparation. This includes project planning, project organization, as well as the determination of project standards. These topics are discussed in the following sections.

Organizational readiness

Getting decision makers on board

An ASAP™ project is doomed to failure if the organization, where it is to be implemented, is not ready to implement SAP. Therefore, one of the first tasks should be to determine if all the key decision makers are on board for the implementation. This step should precede the mobilization of the implementation team's internal and external members.

Management tasks

Management and key decision makers, whose support is critical, should provide a firm commitment that will increase the probability of a successful implementation. They should:

- ❏ Provide top management commitment and support
- ❏ Clearly define project goals and objectives
- ❏ Agree on the different project steps
- ❏ Provide an efficient decision making process
- ❏ Create an environment that is ready for change
- ❏ Setup a team that is qualified and represents the various functional areas

Linking personal and project success

An ASAP™, or even a conventional SAP, project cannot succeed if it lacks management support. With strong backing, a project can move along smoothly and hurdles can be navigated with relative ease. Therefore, it is imperative that management, especially stakeholders, should be intimately involved with the project. They should be made to feel that their own success, or failure, is linked to the success, or failure, of the project.

Project planning

Identifying critical elements

There are a number of steps that need to be taken during the initial (planning) phase of the project. These are the cornerstones upon which the success of a project is built. Weakness in any of these areas can lay the seeds for problems or even outright failure. Therefore, these basic elements should be identified, understood and implemented.

Since the needs and requirements for each project can be different, due to the uniqueness of each business, the list of critical elements can vary from implementation to implementation. The following section lists some critical elements that were considered by one company during the planning phase of its SAP project. However, as noted earlier, most of these elements can be applied during any implementation.

Guiding principles

These are the high-level principles that should be defined at the start of a project. They define and communicate the company's vision. The guiding principles keep the project focused and, in case of conflicts during project implementation, are the basis upon which conflicts are resolved. The following is an example of a set of guiding principles adopted by one company:

- Implement R/3™ standard business processes
- Implement SAP™ R/3® software as an interactive online system
- Focus on customer satisfaction and supporting SAP™ R/3® software business transactions
- Adhere to business basics

Strategic guiding principles

These are the business principles that address lower level strategic issues. By following a strategy that is well defined, it becomes easier for the implementation to achieve its business objectives. The following is an example of a set of strategic guiding principles:

- Implement an integrated enterprise system—not best of breed
- Strive for "out of the box" initial implementation
- First phase implementation:
    - need not replace all the legacy systems' functionality
    - must run the business and be built on an expandable foundation
- Enterprise deployment will require business process changes
- Buy not make, when possible
- Adhere to open standards

- Always wear the company hat first, your functional hat next
- Think globally—enterprise-wide and not just headquarters
- Core modules must be implemented within one year
- Tightly control changes and minimize investment to the legacy environment
- Have clear signoff criteria

Project business drivers

Typically, these are the business drivers for selecting the ERP software for a particular implementation. These drivers are the main contributors to the benefits expected to be achieved by implementing the software. They are the basis, in many cases, for the metrics used to evaluate and compare performance (before and after implementation). The following is an example of a set of project business drivers used by one company:

- Increase customer loyalty
- Improve revenue and earnings growth
- Increase profitability growth
- Improve performance (efficiency)
- Avoid risk due to obsolete computer systems

Budget, standards and metrics

During this phase, a number of other tasks that are usually associated with the start of a project are initiated. For example, the project manager starts to prepare the project plan, budgets, project standards and metrics. The use of various accelerators starts coming into play.

Building the implementation team

Organizational structure and project team authority

Forming the implementation team is an important task during this phase of the project. Typically, the project team consists of:
- Consultants drawn from external organizations
- Internal company employees drawn from various functional areas

The first step involves creating the project's organizational structure and setting up the project team authority, which has the following responsibilities:
- Propose, approve and implement process changes if:
  - required by SAP
  - they support the business objectives
- Define what is in/out of scope; develop and implement a formal change of scope procedure
- Define high and low priorities within functionality
- Escalate issues outside its direct authority to the Steering Committee and senior management for rapid resolution
- Pull in special expertise from functional organizations, when required
- Develop and implement documentation control procedures for the project team

Team membership

For SAP implementations, team membership is split into the following main groups:
- Client personnel; these include:
  - client's employees
  - client's contractors

- Implementation partner/integrator's personnel; these include:
  - employees of the partner company
  - employees of the partner company's sub-contractor(s)

The client's team usually consists of two types of members:
- Core team members: they have to dedicate 100% of their time to the project
- Extended team members: they have to dedicate 20-50% of their time, depending on the project phase, to the project

An assessment is required to determine the internal strength (capability), and availability, of personnel who need to be pulled into the project implementation team. Depending on this assessment, the number and type of external team members/consultants required for the project is determined.

Selecting consultants

It is important that consultants should be selected with a great deal of care. Too many issues can arise if consultants are not properly selected or if they are not adequately monitored and controlled. Problems that can arise include, but are not limited to, the following:
- High turnover due to the integrator's scheduling needs
- Client's requirements take a back seat
- Assignment of consultants with inadequate experience in the functionality being implemented
- Knowledge transfer is negatively impacted
- Excessive travel bills

How teams are organized

The project team is usually organized by modules or functionality. For example, it is usual to have different teams for Finance, Logistics, Sales & Distribution, and Project System. Usually, there are additional teams such as Basis (Infrastructure and System Administration), Quality Assurance, Training, and Communications.

There are two common approaches for organizing the development (programming) group. In the first approach, they are grouped by functional module and, depending on the resource requirements, a couple of developers are assigned to each module. In the second approach, all developers are organized into a single group. This enables all development requests to be routed through a single responsible person, which helps in screening and prioritizing the numerous requests that come in during the life of the project. Another benefit is that depending on the urgency and workload within the different functional modules, a developer can be quickly reassigned to work on a different module that needs additional resources.

Team characteristics

An SAP project team is a large contingent that consists of employees and consultants of varying traits and skill levels. Even though various specific and specialized skill sets are required, the team should collectively have certain characteristics such as the ability to:

- Analyze the impact of the new ERP system on business processes, old and new, across the enterprise
- Analyze functional and implementation requirements
- Design an integrated system
- Provide ongoing knowledge transfer to employees throughout the project

Team building

During the project preparation phase, team-building activities are initiated. In SAP projects, it is important to build a cohesive team whose members understand the overall picture. This task is essential because team members are drawn from diverse groups including internal company employees, integrator's team members and sub-contractors, as well as independent consultants. Additionally, many of the internal team members may never have worked together previously or been exposed to projects of this type and size, which require a unique and different approach.

There are many types of team building activities that are available to such teams. A popular approach is to get the team together for an offsite meeting lasting 2-3 days. During this extended meeting, team members get to know each other. They are made aware of the unique characteristics of the SAP™ R/3® software, business and technical implications, and their interdependence on other team members during implementation. The importance of working as an integrated, mutually dependent, team is highly stressed during such meetings.

Training for team members

In order to introduce the internal team members to SAP functionality and features, they are put through Level I training during the project preparation phase. It is recommended that this training start as early as possible.

Chapter 8
Phase 2 - Business Blueprint

Objective and scope

Analyzing the business

The objective of the second, Business Blueprint, phase of an ASAP™ project is to understand how the company runs its existing business and determine its implementation requirements based on the organization's future needs. For this purpose, a comprehensive analysis of the business is undertaken. This analysis involves understanding the company's business, determining how the existing processes work, and identifying the functionality supported by the existing systems. This is followed by comparing the existing business practices, and functionality, to those supported by SAP.

The blueprint phase analysis also encompasses the identification of existing platforms and applications, interfaces to be developed (to systems that will not be retired and replaced by SAP), bolt-ons required, data migration requirements, etc. Gaps, which refer to existing functionality that an implemented SAP will not support, are also identified.

Interview objectives

During this phase, company executives, managers and other key employees are interviewed extensively. The interviewing is done in individual as

well as group sessions. The questioning is based on a series of template questions. Based on the answers provided, and the discussions that take place during this process, the consultants understand and/or define:
- Company's business
- How the enterprise operates
- Critical elements of the business
- Desired business processes
- Business and functionality requirements
- Implementation scope
- Implementation risks

Based on the knowledge gained during the interview process, the consultants start visualizing how to tailor the feature rich R/3™ software so that it can meet the company's unique requirements.

Reference scope document

At the end of the blueprint phase, a very comprehensive document, called the *Blueprint Document*, is generated and published. The signed-off blueprint document effectively becomes the scope and reference document for the project.

What the blueprint document contains

The blueprint document can be described as the visual model of the enterprise after the SAP™ R/3® software has been implemented. It documents:
- Existing functionality
- Future functionality after SAP implementation
- R/3™ processes currently in operation and those required to run the business in the future
- Implementation scope
- Organizational structure required to implement SAP

- Deferred functionality (to be implemented during a subsequent phase/project)
- Gaps
- Potential risks

The blueprint document, in addition to the items listed previously, also identifies:
- Master data and transaction data
- Data conversion and migration requirements
- Interfaces required to be built
- Legacy systems to be retired
- Bolt-ons required
- Reporting requirements

Training for team members

During the blueprint phase, project team members start Level II training, which involves understanding the R/3™ business processes.

Defining the organizational structure

An important decision reached during the blueprint phase is the definition of the SAP organizational structure based upon the organization's business processes. This structure significantly impacts the way in which SAP is configured to meet the needs of the enterprise. For example, the definition of plants impacts the amount of data entry required, maintenance requirements, reporting and analysis, etc.

Organizational structure characteristics

The organizational structure, as applicable to the SAP model, has the following characteristics:

- Is central to SAP™ R/3® software operation and control
- Needs to be defined before any significant configuration can be done
- Provides the fundamental data and functional architecture within the SAP system
- Enables complex structures
- Structure can be designed based on each company's business processes
- Is flexible, which permits changes to structures
- Flexibility enables separate structures and views for different functional areas such as purchasing, sales and accounting
- Some changes are difficult to implement; others are not feasible even if they are easy to configure because of their significant, and unacceptable, impact on some other functional area(s)
- Enables inter-company processing

Impact of organizational structure

The influence of the SAP organizational structure, which is flexible and can be modified to meet the needs of a changing business, can be far reaching. For example, it can influence how:

- SAP functionality will meet the business requirements
- Inter-company processing will take place
- Reporting and analysis is done

The organizational structure also determines how data is defined in the system, complexity of data input, and the size of the master data files. Therefore, it is highly recommended that the organizational structure be defined as early as possible.

While flexibility permits changes to be made, any changes made after a project is in full swing can potentially be very expensive and also delay the project. Changes to the organizational structure can be made at any stage. However, any late stage changes should be limited to fine tuning only.

Changes permitted when the project is in full swing should typically be due to two reasons only:
- ❏ Business changes have occurred since the structure was defined
- ❏ Existing structure, if implemented, will create major problems

Important elements of the organizational structure
Company code

This is the highest element in the organizational structure. The company code is a legal and organizationally independent unit. It represents an independent accounting unit that has its own financial statements. Its other characteristics are:
- ❏ Produces its own financial documents; generates balance sheet and P&L statement
- ❏ Subsidiaries are usually classified as companies
- ❏ Financial statements for all companies can be consolidated
- ❏ All financial documents are posted at the company level
- ❏ Assignments at the company level include fiscal year, chart of accounts, and accounting currency
- ❏ Limited master data is defined at the company level

Controlling area

This represents an organizational element for which the management of costs and profits can be performed. Its two main elements are:
- ❏ Cost center, which is the basic unit for collecting costs
- ❏ Profit center, which collects revenues and costs (through cost centers)

Business structure

The various functional areas, such as Logistics, Finance and Human Resources, can define their own structures independently. The following are examples of the structure elements in Logistics:

- Plants
- Sales organizations
- Purchasing organizations
- Storage locations

Chapter 9
Phase 3 - Realization

During the realization phase of the ASAP™ roadmap, the Business Blueprint is converted into reality. During this phase, the system is configured, based on the Business Blueprint requirements, and tested. This is not a straightforward process. Rather, the transformation of the company's business requirements into the "to-be" business solution is iterative in nature: build, test, refine and re-test. The following sections describe the realization sub-phases and the various tasks carried out during their implementation.

Simulation

Configuration

In this first configuration step, the consultants quickly configure the preliminary design. This is the baseline system that is based upon the Business Blueprint document. This configuration covers about 80% of the company's business processes and daily business transactions. Configuration typically involves modifying the SAP™ R/3® software through non-programming methods such as changes in SAP baselines settings, flipping switches, modifying table entries, etc. Most of the changes are made through the IMG within the Business Engineer.

Playbacks

After the initial configuration has been completed, the system is demonstrated to selected managers and key members of the end-user community. These playback demonstrations introduce the new software, to a few key employees, and start the process of getting the end-user community on board. It also starts the feedback and iteration process, which ultimately leads to the final configured system. Playbacks are generally performed periodically based on the consultants' preferences and style. Some like to demonstrate the configured functionality on a weekly basis. Others prefer a schedule based on the importance of the process being configured or the completion of a particular process or functionality.

Demonstration of the configured systems and processes is an important step because the end-user community representatives are required to sign-off before the system can be switched on. If they are not involved with the implementation from the beginning, they can impede the signoff process due to legitimate concerns about approving something they are not familiar and comfortable with.

Other tasks

During this phase, project team members obtain in-depth Level II training. They are also initiated in the important task of knowledge transfer, which is required for ensuring that the system will be well run and maintained in the future—after the consultants are gone. This is a task which consultants should be required to perform systematically at every stage of the project, instead of at the end.

Validation

Configuration

During this sub-phase, the design is refined and finalized. The project team fine-tunes the system so that all the business and process requirements are configured. During this phase, the remaining 20% of the business processes and transactions are configured. This phase covers the customization of the company's unique business processes and exceptions. At the end of this phase, a fully configured system becomes available.

Business process procedures

An important task performed during the realization phase is the creation of a business process master list. Team members start writing business process procedures (BPPs), which document the configured system. This documentation can serve three purposes. It can be used:

- For training (without any changes)
- As the template from which the final training documentation is created
- As reference documentation

End-user documentation

The ultimate test of an implementation is the ability of users to use the system effectively. For this, they have to be trained on how to use the SAP application. For effective training, quality end-user training documentation is required. The business process procedures, which are based on individual transactions that need to be executed during operations, usually serve this purpose. However, many companies create additional training documentation for the end-users. Typically, the contract for this task is awarded to specialized training and documentation companies.

Unit and integration testing

Need for testing

No business software can afford to be released into production without extensive testing. A thoroughly tested software can be introduced with minimum pain and disruption and, not surprisingly, is usually accepted quickly. On the other hand, an inadequately tested software can have serious repercussions including the ultimate penalty—being discarded.

Testing an integrated ERP software like SAP is a very challenging task. At the high level, the testing objective for such software is to answer the following questions:

- Are business operations supported by the processes that have been created?
- Is the software performing as configured and expected?
- Is SAP interacting with the external systems as expected?
- Are the performance criteria being met for the various business processes?

The benefits that can be gained by testing thoroughly include:

- Confirmation that the processes work as expected
- Have a configuration that is streamlined
- Performance that can be guaranteed
- Improved integration
- Lower costs
- Reduced risks
- Screening of dirty data, which highlights inadequate data preparation and cleanup

The testing of the implemented software is done in two phases. These are:
- Unit testing
- Integration testing

Unit testing

Every configuration change, even though it may affect only a small part of a business process, needs to be tested. During unit testing, which is the initial testing phase, the focus is on individual transactions. For example, transactions such as creating a vendor, creating a customer, modifying a purchase order, receiving a purchased item into stock, etc., are tested. For each transaction that is expected to be executed, a script or a business process procedure (BPP) is created.

The various transactions are tested in stages/cycles within a specific functional area. With each cycle, the testing becomes more complex. For example, the following is a typical sequence of tests that are conducted in the Materials Management module:
- Create a purchase order for one organization
- Change the purchase order
- Receive goods against the purchase order
- Return partial quantity of goods received
- Create purchase orders for all organizations

This incremental testing in stages can continue to become more complex. However, when the need arises to integrate other functional areas, the second phase of testing, known as integration testing, comes into play.

Integration testing
Business scenarios

After configuration has been completed, a number of business scenarios are developed by the project team, in conjunction with key members of the end-user community, for the purpose of integration testing. These scenarios cover all the business areas that are impacted by the SAP implementation. They also include the testing of interfaces, which are the links between the SAP™ R/3® software and other systems. These links, which can be to disparate systems such as a warehouse system, third-party tax software, bar coding system, etc., can be very complicated and require thorough testing.

Integration testing is usually performed with a process-oriented perspective. For example, a typical scenario will include all the steps required for creating a purchase order—from order entry through shipping and invoicing.

After the business scenarios have been developed, they are thoroughly tested. More the customization of software that is done, greater is the complexity and effort required to perform integration testing.

End-user involvement

To validate the data migrated from the legacy systems, additional resources from the various functional groups are required during the testing phase. During integration testing, the need for end-user involvement is very high. Besides being able to take some load off the core team members, end-users can test the system functionality more thoroughly because they know the company business better than any consultant.

Signoff

A key element in integration testing is end-user sign-off. The signoff process can be quite smooth if the end-users are involved in the testing phase.

Every business scenario needs to be approved and signed-off. End-user acceptance and buy-in should be documented because it prevents complaints from coming in later—after the system becomes operational.

Testing process

There are two ways in which testing is usually performed:

1. A quality assurance (QA) team is organized and made responsible for all testing. This team typically consists of a few core team members plus a few business users drawn from the various functional groups. Each team member is assigned a few business scenarios and made responsible for testing them from end-to-end, i.e., the complete process.
2. Each functional team performs testing within its own functional area. Each tester is responsible for only a small segment of the business process. During testing, when a process moves to another functional area, such as from Purchasing to Finance, the testing responsibility gets shifted to the appropriate functional area. The next tester, from Finance in this case, continues testing from the point where the previous tester, from Purchasing, left off.

The advantage of having multiple testers is that each tester knows his own area very well. Therefore, such a tester can execute and test the business scenarios very quickly. However, in such a case, the knowledge picked up by the team members is limited due to their being exposed to only a few transactions within their own area.

Who does the testing

The amount of testing involved during an SAP implementation can be fairly extensive because it involves executing business scenarios encompassing different functional areas. This leads to the requirement for testers to be drawn from the following groups:

- Full-time project core team members
- Part-time project core team members
- Business users

Data conversions

When the new SAP™ R/3® software is switched on, it cannot be used effectively unless the system has been previously loaded with a large amount of data. The required data includes both transaction data and master data (such as part numbers, purchase orders, sales orders, bill of materials, etc.). Due to the large amount of data that is typically required, and the time and cost involved in keying in this data in SAP, migrating this data from the retiring systems in an efficient manner becomes a necessity.

Factors to consider

The amount and type of data that needs to be migrated into SAP from the legacy systems can vary from implementation to implementation. The factors that determine this include:

- Business necessity
- Type of data (transaction or master data)
- Quantity of data
- Quality of data
- Amount of data cleanup effort required
- Time required for loading
- Constraints due to data loading sequence
- Cost involved
- Complexity of migrating data
- Complexity of business rules to be applied
- Standard or custom programs required
- Availability of ABAP™ and legacy programming resources
- Historical requirements
- Tax and legal requirements
- Reporting requirements
- End-user manpower availability for validation

Data migration methods

There are two basic steps for transferring data into the SAP™ R/3® system. The first is conversion, which requires legacy data to be formatted, into a structure called a flat file, so that the SAP™ R/3® can read it. In the next step, an SAP data transfer program is used to read the flat file and move it into the SAP™ R/3® system. To transfer data, the SAP standard data transfer programs use one of the following methods:

- Batch input: simulates data input by processing the normal screens of the corresponding online transaction
- Direct input: thoroughly checks the flat file before processing it; in the next step, the R/3 database is updated directly

When to start data migration

The data migration effort is often started late during many implementations, which leads to many problems. It is highly advisable that this effort be started as early as possible. Data migration, using small sample data sets, should be practiced frequently before going-live. When this effort is started early, its effectiveness is limited during the initial data loads due to the incomplete system configuration. In many cases, loads fail due to incomplete or changing configuration. However, the benefit of starting early is that it provides valuable experience to the developers. Since data migration and loading is an iterative process, running 2-3 test loads before the system goes live can ensure that the final data load runs smoothly. The test runs also help in determining how long it will take to completely load the SAP production system in the final run.

Which data to migrate

Every enterprise operates differently, collects different data, and has different types of legacy systems. Therefore, each implementation can be expected to have a different grouping of the data that needs to be migrated. The following lists are the master data and transaction data, automated and manual, migrated during one implementation:

Automated master data
- Chart of accounts
- General ledger
- Fixed assets
- Material master
- Customer master
- Price conditions
- Service parts
- Sites and units
- Configurations
- Vendor master
- Purchase order info records
- Routings
- Bill of materials

Manual master data
- Cost centers/departments
- Work centers
- Sales pricing/discounts condition tables
- Customer material info records
- Templates for product proposals
- Sales employees

Automated transaction data
- ❏ General ledger balances
- ❏ Open accounts payable
- ❏ Open accounts receivable
- ❏ Open quotations
- ❏ Open sales orders
- ❏ Service contracts
- ❏ Field service reports
- ❏ Open service calls
- ❏ Inventory quantities
- ❏ Consumption history

Manual transaction data
- ❏ Open production orders
- ❏ Open quotations

Data cleanup

Why dirty data is an issue

A common problem is that the issue of dirty data is ignored or it is not given sufficient importance. Therefore, the cost and effort required to perform this task is frequently underestimated. In many cases, data quality is given scant attention until it starts creating serious issues in the SAP production system. When that happens, it seriously impact business and usually requires crisis handling.

What cleanup involves

Even if the legacy data is clean to start with, it may need to be modified or filtered before it is loaded into SAP. For example:

- There can be a mismatch in the parts numbering scheme (alpha versus numeric)
- The number of characters used for identifying existing parts may be in excess of what SAP allows
- Vendors that have been inactive for a certain period, such as 24 months, may need to be filtered out

Another common problem is duplication: an existing customer might be having multiple entries, such as IBM and International Business Machines. This would indicate that there are two customers instead of only one. Such issues require that the data be filtered and modified—by changing field length, type, etc.,—before it is moved into SAP from the legacy system.

Where is the data checked

The data that is migrated into SAP needs to be clean and validated. There are two options available for ensuring that only clean data resides in SAP when it goes live. These are:

- Cleanup on the legacy system side before loading (at the source)
- Cleanup on the SAP side after loading (at the target)

In the first case, most of the cleanup effort takes place on the legacy side. After end-users validate the data, it is loaded into SAP. On the SAP side, validation is done by the system during the loading process. Subsequently, after loading has been completed, data owners check and validate the master data and transaction data to ensure that the migrated data is clean.

In the second case, minimal checking is performed on the legacy side. It is expected that the validation rules enforced by SAP, during loading, will prevent most of the bad data from coming in. After it has been loaded into SAP, the migrated data is cleaned, if required, and validated by the functional team members and key business users.

Who needs to validate migrated data

It should be emphasized that the technical resources, i.e., ABAP™ and legacy programmers, should not be relied upon to check and validate business data. It should be the responsibility of the end-users to validate such data because they own, and know, this data very well.

Tools available

A number of data conversion tools from companies like Conversion Sciences, which uses a proprietary R/3™ data conversion tool called Proteus, and ETI are available. They can be useful in reducing data migration costs.

Interfaces, enhancements and reports

Interfaces

The introduction of SAP into an enterprise typically results in the retirement of many, though not all, legacy systems. To ensure that the remaining systems and bolt-ons talk to SAP, either in one-way or two-way mode, interfaces need to be built. In some cases, SAP provides a generic interface to its own software. The coding requirements for interfaces are not very complicated or extensive. However, they do require knowledge of the legacy systems being retired.

A lot of time and effort is involved in building and testing interfaces. Their development can require highly skilled and technical resources. Also, a significant part of integration testing involves testing interfaces. Therefore, early identification of the interfaces to be built can ensure that their development starts early on in the project, which ensures early completion. This enables thorough testing without decreasing the effectiveness of the testing by reducing the scope of testing that, typically, occurs when interface development falls behind schedule.

Enhancements

In order to accommodate the specific needs at every implementation, a number of custom enhancements are needed. These can range from a few for a vanilla implementation to many for a more customized implementation. Some enhancements can be very simple, while others can be fairly complex, especially if an attempt is made to mirror the retiring legacy systems environment.

Enhancements can require significant ABAP™ resources, testing, and SAP source code modifications. A major disadvantage associated with an enhancement is that it will always require special attention and testing every time an SAP release or upgrade is implemented. However, the advantage is that enhancements can make certain processes run more smoothly. Therefore, every enhancement request should be carefully evaluated before a decision is made to proceed with it.

Reports

Reporting should be an important element in every SAP implementation. However, it is often neglected. The reason is that the primary implementation objective is to make the software run the business. In some implementations, serious consideration is given to reporting only after going live. Consequently, after the system is put into production at these sites, there exists a crisis-like atmosphere because many users cannot get their work done due to the unavailability of critical reports and information.

Reporting requirements need to be addressed as early as possible. The process should be started by listing all the existing legacy reports. These should be grouped by priority. Business critical ones should be identified, and worked upon, as early as possible. If an SAP report that matches a critical legacy report does not exist, then a custom report can be justified and developed. If early identification of these reports is done, it can enable more efficient allocation and utilization of ABAP™ resources for developing custom reports.

Creating SAP reports can be very complicated and tedious because the SAP data schema is extremely complex and the relationships between tables are not easy to determine. Using custom ABAP/4® programming to create reports can be very expensive due to the high rates charged by skilled ABAP™ developers. Therefore, custom development of reports should be discouraged, especially those requested due to personal preferences, unless they are justified for business reasons.

Chapter 10
Phase 4 - Final Preparation

During the final preparation phase of an ASAP™ project, the following tasks are performed:
- ❏ Refine the system
- ❏ Prepare go-live plan
- ❏ End-user training
- ❏ Knowledge transfer
- ❏ System administration
- ❏ Data migration
- ❏ Final testing and fine tuning

Preparing for the home stretch

Refining the system

During this stage, the system is refined, adjusted and tweaked. Configuration, interfaces and processes are adjusted. Changes are initiated due to end-user testing and feedback, modifications in procedures and/or processes, unit and integration testing, change in scope and/or requirements, etc.

During this phase, the system continues to undergo testing. As interfaces get completed, they are tested. Every process touched by a change, such as the introduction of a new interface or a configuration change, is tested and/or retested. Every change made needs to be tested because it has the potential to create a problem, including breaking a process, due to the integrated nature of the software.

Prepare go-live plan
Cutover plan

In this step, a plan is prepared and implemented to switch over to the SAP system from the retiring legacy systems. This plan, better known as the cutover plan, includes all the major activities and tasks that are required to be executed during the last few weeks prior to go-live. A well-prepared and realistic cutover plan ensures a smooth transition to the SAP production system. A typical cutover plan includes:

- Activities and tasks
- Schedule and milestones
- Data load sequence with estimated time for each sub-load
- Assignment of the person responsible for each task
- Schedule and procedure for shutting down the legacy systems
- Data cleanup procedure
- Reconciliation procedure
- Checklist for reviewing readiness

Important elements of the cutover plan

The cutover plan lists every type of data load to be executed. It also includes the relationship of each data load item to other data loads items, i.e., successor and predecessor relationships, if applicable.

In accordance with the loading schedule, it needs to be ensured that the business users responsible for data cleanup and validation are made available to the project team. This scheduling is very important for sequential data item loads because the window available, between the completion of one data item load and the start of the next item to be loaded, can be very small. During the short periods available between various data item loads, the loaded data needs to be checked and validated quickly. If this is not done within the allocated time period, it can either delay the overall loading process or, if the checking is incomplete or sloppy, lead to production problems after go-live.

The cutover plan needs to ensure that a small window is provided between the time data loading is completed and the system is turned on. This window, of half to one day, is required for taking care of any last minute unexpected problems.

Plan approval

The cutover plan should be reviewed by project management, technical team leads, business leads, corporate senior management as well as the Steering Committee. Once it has been approved, its effective implementation as per the plan can ensure that the go-live experience will not be chaotic.

Preparing the users and support staff

How much to spend on training

A rule of thumb is that training should make up at least 10% of the overall implementation budget. Of this amount, at least 1% should be earmarked for training the company executives. Unfortunately, during SAP implementations, training is often neglected. The results of inadequate training are usually manifested, sooner or later, with serious repercussions at times.

End-user training

This is an important part of an SAP implementation that takes place during the final preparation phase. Training is one of the factors evaluated

while making the go/no-go decision prior to going live because it has a considerable impact on:
- Smoothness of transition to the new system
- End-user acceptance
- Overall project success

Why training is required

An SAP project introduces massive changes within an organization. It can force workers to change the way they do their jobs due to procedure and process changes, role changes, etc. With its introduction, many jobs are eliminated or redefined and new roles are created. Users need to retrain and learn new skills, procedures and processes. They need to learn how their actions can impact others in an integrated system. Therefore, if training is not provided effectively to the people who will ultimately use the system, it can cause serious operational and morale problems.

End-users needing SAP to perform their jobs start attending Level I and Level II training during this phase. However, implementation team members, who are fairly experienced by now, attend Level II and Level III training during this phase.

Who needs to be trained

There exists a need for training throughout the life of an SAP project. Both project team members and end-users require this training. Project team members start getting their initial training during the project planning and blueprint phases. Training continues into the realization phase. However, during the final preparation phase, the training focus shifts to the business community—the end-users.

Training scope and cost

The scope of training can be very daunting, especially if the end-users, who can number in the thousands, are scattered across different parts of the country or the globe. Training expenses can be fairly high because:

- Users need to learn new procedures and processes
- Many job roles and responsibilities change
- Practically every user has to be trained

The impact of inadequate end-user training can be very serious. Therefore, training should be approached with a well-planned strategy. The following are some facts that have been observed about end-user training, which need to be considered by those planning such training:

- Training expenses are high
- Training cost is consistently underestimated
- Training budget gets cut whenever project budgets are squeezed
- Training cost can range from 10-15% of the project budget

Training materials

The following are some tips applicable to training materials:

- Plan early: have a training plan in place, as soon as possible, for all potential users
- Hire professionals to create user-friendly materials
- Discard the view that training materials cannot be created until configuration and testing have been completed
- Do not use configuration scripts for end-user training

Time constraint

The biggest training challenge is to train all the users within a very short period. If the training is staggered over an extended period, the first few groups of end-users getting trained will not be able to use their newly gained knowledge right away. In most cases, they will require refresher training prior to going live. This can be an issue since the number of SAP trainers is limited and there can be hundreds, even thousands, of end-users who need to be trained.

A fairly successful method employed widely is to train, as early as possible, a group of power users who are drawn from the business community. After they have been trained, power users can train other end-users within their own functional areas.

The overall training strategy and plan should be publicized as early as possible. This permits efficient scheduling and the creation of high quality, well organized, training materials that are well received by the end-user community.

Knowledge transfer

As implementation proceeds at a site, the consultants thoroughly learn the business processes and configuration specifics for that installation. Unfortunately, from the company's perspective, this knowledge is lost once the consultants leave. Therefore, it becomes imperative for the installation specific knowledge gained by the consultants to be transferred to the company's employees. This needs to be done through a clearly laid out knowledge transfer plan.

Who should perform knowledge transfer

The main technical drivers and leaders during an SAP implementation are the consultants. The client's employees do not have SAP relevant knowledge to fully understand what is going on—till rather late in the project. By that stage, most of the configuration has already been done and new business processes established. Therefore, they have limited knowledge about most areas and, in many cases, end up knowing practically nothing about how the system was configured and implemented. Hence, the only ones capable of transferring knowledge are the consultants.

Why knowledge transfer is ignored

The implementation team at most SAP projects is primarily focused on the implementation rather than on running the system after go-live—when the lack of knowledge transfer starts to manifest itself in many ways. Therefore, management should make knowledge transfer a high priority item. It should ensure that the consultants consistently and systematically document what they have done throughout the project.

The tendency, at too many projects, has been to ask the consultants to document what they have configured too late—only at the end of the project. The problem with this approach is that during the final preparation and post go-live phases, consultants are too busy resolving issues and fighting fires. At that stage, it is also highly likely that they have forgotten the specific details of what they did months earlier. Therefore, any documentation that they provide at the end of the project contains skimpy details at best which, in most cases, is inadequate for supporting the system after go-live.

What needs to be done

It is imperative that there should be a systematic method for knowledge transfer from the consultants to the client's employees on the project team. The process, methodology and schedule for this should be defined as early as possible during the project. The ideal method is to assign a team member to every consultant right from the start of the project. This buddy system ensures that maximum knowledge is absorbed and retained by the company staff.

Getting ready to throw the switch

System administration

The technical (Basis) team conducts system tests during this phase. Stress and performance tests are conducted on the servers and other hardware. Auxiliary systems are checked and the system is fine tuned and readied for production.

Data migration

As per the cutover plan schedule, the remaining business data is now migrated, in a step-by-step manner, to the new system. The migrated data is validated after it is imported into the new system. If the legacy system continues to remain in operation for a few extra days after its data has been migrated, any new transactions recorded there are keyed in manually in the SAP system. This duplication of entries ensures that no data fails to be available in the SAP system after it goes live.

Final testing and fine tuning

During final preparation, the system continues to be tested and fine-tuned. The system is subjected to volume and stress tests, performance is optimized, and the system is readied for production. Integration tests are conducted, converted/migrated data is verified, and interfaces are checked. Peripheral equipment, such as printers, bar code readers, etc., are tested.

SAP's Going Live Check can also be performed at this stage. This enables SAP experts to login remotely, analyze the configuration, and make recommendations for optimizing the system.

Chapter 11
Phase 5 - Go-Live & Support

Final check before take-off

Readiness assessment

An SAP implementation project is long and challenging. It aims to achieve a lot—to get rid of a number of existing legacy systems and replace them by a single system. However, before the switch can be turned on, it needs to be determined whether the SAP system and the business are ready for the big change. For the final decision to proceed, a go/no-go evaluation is required, which depends on a number of factors. The typical factors to be considered, and questions to be asked, before the go/no-go decision can be made are the following:

- ❑ Are the processes supported?
- ❑ Has migration been completed and are the interfaces ready?
- ❑ Has the migrated data been validated and reconciled with the legacy system?
- ❑ What is the status of the development effort?
- ❑ Has integration testing been completed satisfactorily?
- ❑ Are the business critical reports and forms ready?
- ❑ Have the users been trained and ready to run the system?
- ❑ Are there any identifiable showstoppers?

Operational support

This needs to be organized well in advance of the go-live date. Typical support encompasses resolution of problems and bugs, requests for enhancements, and training. The largest number of support calls logged immediately after go-live typically deal with authorization issues. To handle support calls, an issue tracking mechanism is required. Companies use various third party software, such as Vantive and Remedy, for this purpose.

To ensure an efficient mechanism for handling support issues, they should be segregated into three areas: problems, enhancements, and reports. This permits a focused and methodical approach for handling the large number of issues that can arise and require prioritization. It also helps in tracking metrics.

Change controls

Even before the system is turned on, any changes that are requested should be put through a strict change control process. Change control procedures ensure that changes to business processes, configuration and programs are implemented systematically in a controlled environment.

Change control procedures also ensure that any changes made to the system, and released as "transports", pass through a verification process. Such procedures dictate that any changes to be implemented in the production client are first tested elsewhere, in another client(s), and have the proper release authorization. Having a documented change control procedure ensures that any problem caused by a released transport can be traced quickly and followed by corrective action or, if required, a reversal of the change that was implemented.

Communication
Where it is required

In an SAP project, which is implemented by scores of project team members, and impacts hundreds of users, there is a lot more to be done than just configuring and implementing the software package. Many other tasks need to be performed including effective and regular communication at every stage of the project. For example, communication is required between:

- Project team members
- Project management and team members
- Project management and the Steering Committee
- Project management and business management
- Project team members and the end-user community
- Business management and end-users

Communications targeted towards the end-users are very important. Typically, most end-users have no idea about the scope and impact of the SAP project. Most view SAP as just another software that can be learned on the fly. However, such an attitude can cause serious problems. If this perception is not changed, many users will ultimately find out, after go-live, that they are unable to perform their jobs. Therefore, end-users need to be educated about the impending changes, especially those impacting business procedures, their roles and responsibilities, and individual training requirements.

What needs to be communicated

Communication is required during all stages of the project. For end-users, a special effort must be made to keep them informed. Communications targeting end-users should be focused on, though not limited to, the following:

- Why SAP is being implemented
- Importance of the software change to the enterprise
- Impact of changeover to the new software
- Status of the project
- Creating awareness about changing jobs and roles

- Managing user expectations, especially the view that SAP is a cure-all for the company's problems
- Quashing rumors and negative opinions, if perceived, about the project
- Need and schedule for new training
- Informing them about the impending rollout of the software

Security
Why security is required

The integrated nature of SAP™ R/3® software enables users to have access to information that was previously available in the legacy system to only a few select employees. This creates security and confidentiality issues. For example, personnel and salary data is very sensitive. Therefore, this creates the requirement to provide access to end-users based on authorization profiles that, typically, are based on job functions. This limits the amount of navigation that anyone can perform in the system.

How authorization profiles are created

An authorization profile can be based on a combination of transaction codes or various SAP objects. Typically, a profile is based on a role, which is based on job mapping.

In the first step, the various jobs required to run the business are identified. In the next step, an authorization profile is assigned to each job. Therefore, when a user is assigned an appropriate authorization profile, it permits him to perform only those transactions that are included in that profile. The background work involved in setting up a variety of authorization profiles, for thousands of users, can be significant and requires careful planning.

Balancing security and access needs

The conflicting security and access requirements raises the question of where the line should be drawn between security and empowerment. Having a restrictive security authorization policy makes employees less empowered and less productive. However, having a wide-open policy can create serious problems. Besides sensitivity and confidentiality issues, a lax authorization policy can allow users to navigate to, and change, data that they are not supposed to.

SAP support

A number of avenues are available for obtaining the support of the SAP organization. These include the Online Service System (OSS) and EarlyWatch™ service.

Online Service System

This is the first-level service provided by SAP that can be accessed remotely by its customers. Using a remote login, a user can query a huge database maintained by SAP. This database contains the thousands of issues that SAP users have faced, over the years, and resolved. It also contains the latest news about releases, SAP news, installation and upgrade information, training, etc.

If an answer to a problem is not found in the OSS database, the user can log the issue in the database. SAP experts then address the problem. During the period that a logged issue is open, a user can track its progress. When a problem is finally resolved, its solution becomes available to all SAP users accessing the OSS.

The Online Service System can also be accessed through the Internet. When it is accessed through this mode, OSS is known as SAPNet.

EarlyWatch™

This is a proactive service that allows SAP to diagnose a system so that potential problems can be recognized early on and, consequently, permit them to be resolved before they become real issues.

Thinking beyond go-live

Organization structure

The organizational structures required to implement and operate SAP are, due to the nature of their different needs and requirements, quite different. Most enterprises implement SAP projects without seriously thinking about how the post go-live organization should be structured until rather late in the project implementation cycle. The assumption under which many companies operate during implementation, that operations can be handled after go-live in the usual manner with the existing setup, is wrong. After the SAP switch is turned on, life is never the same for the employees who previously ran the business using the legacy systems.

A new organizational structure should be created, as early as possible, to reflect the future operational needs of the company. One such need is the significant support capability required to be put in place. This can be created around the nucleus of the project core team and the existing IT support organization. A feature of the new organization is that it is flatter—with fewer managers. Also, since technical resources with the skills required to support SAP functionality are difficult to find, a fair number of consultants will typically need to be retained at the end of the implementation to ensure adequate staffing.

Change control procedure

No SAP implementation can ever remain static. Even after go-live, the software continues to be modified. The changes can be minor if a very customized implementation took place—because relatively few changes are required post go-live. However, the changes can be very extensive at a vanilla implementation site due to the pent-up demand for customization.

Besides requests for enhancements and the addition of new functionality, a company also has to deal with the periodic release and upgrade cycle of the SAP™ R/3® software. Therefore, a sound change control procedure needs to be defined and implemented. The change control process should clearly layout the procedures for implementing changes to processes, procedures and systems.

Staffing

One of the biggest challenges faced by organizations after going live is to retain the core team members who picked up specialized skills during the project. With skilled SAP personnel in high demand, it is not unusual to have a 30% turnover in this group after a project is completed. Therefore, a company needs to have a good retention program so that it avoids losing talent at the end of its SAP project. A number of methods have been used to achieve this. These include giving more responsibilities, absorption in other groups who are working on more challenging projects (such as e-Commerce), increased monetary benefits, lateral move within the SAP group, etc. Companies that have recognized the potential turnover issue early on have managed to retain a high percentage of their project team members.

Chapter 12
Project principles, guidelines and tips

All software and/or application projects, such as SAP and Data Warehousing, have some common elements such as planning and preparation, execution and control. Therefore, many of the basic principles of project management can be applied to all of them. However, ERP and SAP projects are characterized by many unique elements that set them apart from conventional projects. These unique characteristics are described in the following sections.

Factors to consider before starting the project

Why is the project being undertaken

It should be understood why the project is being undertaken and what management expects from its implementation. The following are some questions that can provide useful insight into this:

- Is the objective the improvement of already efficient and streamlined procedures and processes?
- Is the objective the replacement of inadequate systems?
- Is everything in disarray or are only a couple of problem systems the drivers for change?
- Is an attempt being made to fix everything simultaneously?

Project justification

Project justification should precede every software project. For all SAP projects, since they are so massive in scope, it is imperative that a thorough cost/benefit analysis be performed. It sounds incredible but cost/benefit analysis have been performed after ERP projects have already been awarded, including one on which this author worked.

Cost/benefit analysis should be performed by someone who has high credibility within the company or by a consulting company experienced in SAP implementations. This can defuse any criticism that the project is being implemented for some executive's personal agenda. A well-justified project ensures that employees will believe that the project is worthwhile. In general, the best justifications match the business objectives of the enterprise to the project goals.

The project justification should be communicated effectively to a selectively targeted audience. It helps to be candid. For example, at one implementation, it was clearly communicated that an important reason for undertaking the ERP project was competition. The company's two competitors had already implemented SAP and therefore, in order to remain competitive, it had to buy an expensive ERP system. This candidness did help in getting support from some groups that, initially, had some reservations about the project.

Has the business strategy been defined

This needs to be done prior to software selection and implementation. By performing this task, the company's strategic and business objectives have a greater chance of being met. It also helps to provide a competitive advantage or, at worst, place the company on an equal footing with the competition.

How will the SAP system be used

It needs to be understood how the SAP system will fit in the overall technical architecture and business strategy. The inputs for this analysis can be quite varied. They can include supply chain software, web-enabled remote access, business intelligence roadmap and data warehousing plans, planned mergers and acquisitions, etc. Companies that give higher priority to strategic business objectives compared to software selection and implementation improve their chances of success considerably.

Readiness assessment

An assessment needs to be made that the organization is ready for the SAP system, which will dramatically change the way business is currently being run. It needs to be determined whether the company is up to the challenge. An assessment also needs to be made to determine management objectives and commitment to the project. If commitment is lacking, or the objectives are not in sync with what the SAP™ R/3® software generally aims to achieve, it is advisable to delay the project until such conditions exist.

Skills assessment

An SAP project should not be initiated without thorough preparation and groundwork. Management should determine the skill levels and capabilities of its employees for selecting the software as well as implementing it. Too often, management is less than well informed and has no idea of the considerable impact that an SAP implementation can have on the organization (during and after implementation).

A careful evaluation is required to determine whether sufficient skills exist in-house to implement the project and, subsequently, operate and maintain the system. A widespread view is that external consultants can fill the gap, which is an erroneous assumption. While there exist thousands of SAP consultants, the ones available for the project being considered may not be adequately qualified.

While business needs and requirements drive the push for ERP technology, the role of the support organization, the IT department, cannot be ignored. Since it is critical to the effort to improve and support business process changes, the skills and resources available within this group should be carefully assessed.

Decision making capabilities

During all stages of an SAP project, critical decisions need to be made. These decisions can significantly influence the way business is conducted after the software has been implemented. Therefore, management must assess the background, temperament and decision making capability of the project staff that will be entrusted with making important decisions. Two critical skills to be evaluated include the ability of these personnel to act quickly and work effectively under stress. In SAP projects, where the stress level is fairly high and teams are highly interdependent, slow decision-making can impact other teams and delay the project.

Specifying the ground rules for decision-making right at the beginning can help ensure success for the implementation. The following are a few rules that can be laid out:

- Project manager to be assigned specific responsibilities
- Project manager must approve any scope or program changes
- Consultants cannot override managers
- Committees will have override authority vis-à-vis individual managers
- No decision to remain pending for more than 48 hours
- No re-direction of blame to third-parties
- Failure responsibility to be shared by the whole team

IT transition ability

An agile and responsive IT organization must be in place to support the rapid pace and requirements of an SAP implementation. If these characteristics are lacking, it needs to be assessed whether a dynamic team can be quickly put together. The risks associated with having a mediocre IT organization, which cannot transition quickly and effectively to the new technology and infrastructure, are very high.

Corporate culture

SAP, which is the most complex project that a company implements, initiates major changes by:

- ❏ Changing the way business is run
- ❏ Changing confusion into coherence by switching from disparate systems to a single system
- ❏ Changing the way people work
- ❏ Empowering employees

All these factors can cause management as well as lower level staff to resist change. Resistance to change is a natural phenomenon. The way companies deal with it is determined, to a large extent, by the corporate culture.

Corporate culture is a good indicator of whether a requirement for success is present. A negative corporate culture can be powerful enough to reduce the chances of success for an SAP project. Therefore, this factor should be evaluated to determine its contribution to the overall project risk.

It should be realized that corporate culture is an extension of management. If management attitude is not positive, it is highly unlikely that an enterprise will change itself just to make an SAP project succeed. Management must have a good understanding of the culture that permeates throughout the organization. It needs to understand its strengths and weaknesses and, based on its analysis, develop an implementation plan that avoids the obvious pitfalls.

Management and implementation

The degree of success that a project achieves is influenced by a number of key indicators. These include the following:

- ❏ Project manager: does he have sufficient responsibility and authority? Is he powerful, respected and experienced?
- ❏ Support: can top management be expected to provide unwavering support during rough times?
- ❏ Goals: can managers work towards corporate goals with the same fervor as with personal goals?
- ❏ Responsibility: will both failures and successes be shared?
- ❏ Resources: can adequate resources be drawn upon?
- ❏ Conflicts: is quick resolution encouraged?
- ❏ Teamwork: does the business environment encourage teamwork over individual achievements?

It is not realistic to expect positive answers to all these questions since few organizations will respond positively to all of them. However, what is important for project success is to understand how the company will deal with each of these issues.

Laying the foundations

Defining the guiding principles

These are the basic principles that need to be defined right at the beginning of the project. They provide the project team with a set of goals that can be referred to throughout the implementation. At times of conflict, between team members or with business users, these principles serve as guidelines. Anything out of alignment with these principles should be discarded or implemented only after obtaining special approval—as an exception due to business or other necessity.

Identifying the business drivers

The project business drivers are specific elements that need to be identified at the start of the project. Besides identifying and clarifying project objectives, they can be used as the basis for metrics used to evaluate the success of the project in meeting its quantitative objectives. Examples of these include increased customer loyalty, revenue and profitability growth, and efficiency improvement.

Obtaining sponsorship

An SAP project needs a sponsor. The project sponsor should be from top management, preferably at the vice president level, and be associated with the department that expects to reap the maximum benefit from the SAP implementation. The sponsor should be an individual who can make things happen and ensure that:

- Management stake in the project is conveyed to all levels
- Top management support is maintained throughout the project
- Necessary resources are provided at critical junctures
- Parties at loggerheads are brought together and, if necessary, force compromises
- Decisions and compromises are enforced

Obtaining management commitment

Management needs to be involved in all project phases—from the pre-implementation phase through to the acceptance of the system. It has to believe in the project, be supportive, and provide significant commitment for a successful implementation. Management must communicate its commitment and associate its own success or failure with the success or failure of the SAP project.

Recognizing the decision makers

It should be ensured that those in management who can influence project success are closely involved with the project. The most important ones should be included in the Steering Committee. The tasks that a Steering

Committee performs include approving the project scope, prioritizing, resolving conflicts and disputes, committing and making available project resources, and monitoring implementation progress. It can provide a key ingredient for effective decision making by empowering the team.

The Steering Committee interacts with the project on a regular basis and can set the direction, which can make or break the project. If the committee is strong, its support can be crucial for project success.

Choosing the implementation leader

The implementation should be led by a senior executive who is decisive and can make things happen. Besides leadership qualities, such an executive should have a good track record of completing projects on time and within budget. Although it is required that the project be led by a strong project manager, the Steering Committee should have the authority to overrule him.

Chapter 13
Factors impacting project success

Many factors come into play during the implementation of an SAP project. The importance of each variable, which depends on the particular installation, can be influenced by the presence or absence of other variables. The factors that are usually ranked high are described in the following sections.

Planning

Organization and management readiness

An organization as well as its management must be committed. They must be ready to introduce changes that, in an SAP project, can be of re-engineering magnitude. Management must be willing to relinquish control. It must be ready to delegate responsibility and empower the project team.

Effective project planning

A realistic project plan is the foundation upon which an implementation is built. It is amazing to find SAP projects being executed without detailed project plans and schedules in place. A project plan with a realistic schedule, milestones and dependencies must be created and publicized at the very start of the project. Where possible, resources should be assigned to specific tasks in the detailed project plan, which ensures ownership and specific responsibilities.

Project team organization
Organization of project teams
An SAP project team typically has the matrix type structure. Such a flat organization is typically organized into teams, such as:
- Functional (FI, MM, PP, etc.)
- Basis/Infrastructure
- Training
- Communication
- Development

Employees or consultants
The first choice for each position within the project organization are company employees. Any open positions, after available employees have been drafted, are filled by hiring new employees or by recruiting consultants. When consultants are hired, it should be confirmed that they are available for the full duration of the project, or for at least the most important phases, because consultant turnover can negatively impact the project in many ways.

When hiring new employees for the project, it is recommended that those with previous SAP experience be given preference. This ensures that consultants have experienced employees looking over their shoulders. While consultants bring a lot of experience to the project, too often, they tend to do what is expedient for them rather than what is in the best interest of the company.

Project team characteristics
Characteristics of team members

Team selection is an important element that can influence the chances of project success. Therefore, assembling a dynamic team should be given high priority. The team members, who should be high caliber professionals, must have the following characteristics:

- Be motivated and ambitious
- Have good functional knowledge
- Have good decision making capability
- Be willing to work long hours
- Be able to work under pressure
- Be able to act quickly
- Work as team players

Ability to think out of the box

During an SAP project, one can frequently hear the words "because we have always done it this way." Typically, this is said in response to questions aimed at determining why something had been done inefficiently, or inexplicably, in the past. This type of response requires the ability to think creatively, out of the box, and recommend changes that will significantly improve the existing way of doing business.

Team members should have the capability of challenging the old methods of doing business, processes and procedures, methods and techniques, etc. Their original thinking needs to be encouraged.

Controls

Effective controls

One of the most important elements in keeping any project on track is to have controls in place. These are the tools that prevent a project from going off track: causing delays, cost overruns and scope creep. For this purpose, standard project management controls can be applied. However, focus on some additional controls can be quite useful during SAP projects. These include control over consultants' turnover, enforcement of escalation rules for decision making, travel costs—which can balloon if a large number of consultants from other locations are assigned to the project, scope control, etc. The areas where costs are likely to overshoot, and are good candidates for control measures, include:

- Maintenance and updates
- Integration testing
- Data conversion
- Consulting
- Training
- Project team salaries (to keep the team intact)

Project manager's background

As in any large IT project, the role of the project manager is important. However, in an SAP project, the stakes are even higher because such a project is critical for the enterprise in many ways.

The project manager needs to be very committed. He should preferably be drawn from an area that is impacted the most by the implementation, which ensures a strong vested interest. The project manager should be respected and have the experience and capability that is trusted within the company. He should also be powerful, which ensures that things can get done when required.

Scope creep
Understanding scope creep

Scope creep is the bane of SAP projects. The tendency during many implementations is to try to mirror the existing features of the legacy systems, which end-users are used to. Also, small and innocuous requests turn into stealth projects, which end up draining valuable resources. In many cases, such projects create integration problems because the other teams are not in the information loop till rather late in the game. Also, many of the typical requests for enhancements and changes, which involve scope creep, need custom development. Such requests require ABAP™ programming resources, which can be very expensive.

Setting rules

The rules for controlling scope should be very strict: nothing can be implemented unless it is specified in the Business Blueprint document. If there is a business critical need that has not been addressed in the blueprint, a scope change request should be initiated and routed through the approval process. At the very least, it must be approved by the team leaders and, depending on the escalation rules, Steering Committee approval may also be required.

It should be communicated, to all concerned, that differentiation should be made between needs and wants. Setting initial rules and enforcing them can help keep everyone on track. For example, at one implementation, it was specified in the blueprint document that the development team would create a total of 20 custom forms and reports. The users were told to prioritize and select for development only 20 forms and reports, that they deemed most business-critical, from among the large number of existing legacy forms and reports.

Months into the project, some users wanted to reclassify a few previously discarded reports as critical. However, they were told that new reports could be included in the 20 most critical list only if an equal number of reports, currently classified as critical, were dropped from the development queue. This control mechanism forced the users to think really hard about prioritization and, consequently, scope creep was avoided in this area.

Requests that are important, but not critical, can be handled by including them in a wait-list queue. These requests can be implemented during a later phase of the project or a few months after go-live (if no additional phase is contemplated in the near future).

Technical

Client architecture
Impact of client architecture
The client architecture impacts:
- Data migration plan
- Data load testing
- Transport path, which refers to the SAP method of duplicating a change made in one client through to all the other clients
- Backup and client refresh strategy
- Development
- Unit and integration testing
- Performance

Undefined architecture
A fairly widespread problem during implementations is that the SAP client architecture is not clearly defined for too long and, consequently, is

not structured efficiently. In many cases, the client architecture gets defined late in the project—when major problems force serious thinking about this issue. At that stage, it becomes very difficult to make major changes without creating a lot of disruption.

If late changes to the client architecture are made, additional work is created due to its impact on data migration and the need to verify that the configuration is still in sync between different clients. This issue requires that a well-planned client architecture be rolled out at the beginning so that only minor changes and tweaking are required during the later project stages.

Early start to data migration

Data migration requires a huge effort. It should be started as early as possible so that, ideally, the team gets an opportunity to test data loading at least 3-5 times before the final load is performed in the production client. Starting early has it drawbacks because the configuration is anything but finalized in the early phases of the project. Therefore, the load routines need to be changed frequently in order to keep them in sync with the changing configuration. However, the advantage is that the team becomes more experienced with each test load. Consequently, the final load, which comes at a critical juncture, becomes a routine task for the experienced developers.

Thorough integration testing

Integration testing is one of the most important phases of an SAP project. The thoroughness and methodical approach used for integration testing is an important factor that determines whether the transition to SAP will be smooth or rocky.

The development effort should be started as early as possible and completed before integration testing starts. One of the worst mistakes that companies make is to continue development while integration testing is in progress. This is an issue because every development change has the potential to impact the system and, therefore, cause confidence in the completed tests to be lost. Hence, to reinstate confidence in the test results, regression testing needs to be done. If regression testing is performed, it lengthens the testing period and the project can easily be delayed. If regression testing is not done, it increases the operational risks following go-live.

Integration testing should be performed using business scenarios that are very comprehensive. They should reflect the way the company's business is going to be run in the future after SAP has been implemented. Such scenarios can easily expose broken processes during the testing phase. Using scenarios that do not span a complete process should be avoided.

Data cleanup responsibility

The data residing in the legacy systems, both master data and transaction data, needs to be migrated to SAP. There are two places where this data can be checked:

- Legacy side (before migration)
- SAP side (after migration)

It is very important that the migrated data be checked thoroughly. If it is not validated, it has the potential to wreak havoc—such as shutting down production lines, incorrectly pricing sales orders, etc. Usually, the business users and extended team members are assigned the data cleanup task. However, due to their being unaware of the implications of bad data getting into the system, and time constraints, they often perform an inadequate job. It is imperative that the importance of data cleanup be conveyed to the personnel responsible for this effort.

Miscellaneous

Responsibility and ownership

Users need to be involved with the project as early as possible. They need to be made aware of the impending changes for the enterprise. It pays to show them functionality as it is configured so that valuable feedback, and suggestions for improvement, can be obtained continuously. By being involved from the start, important users are not surprised when the system goes live. It also gives the project team members an opportunity to manage user expectations. Another advantage is that the signoff process becomes relatively smooth.

Knowledge transfer
Why transfer knowledge does not occur

There is little time to relax during an SAP implementation. Every deadline and milestone is followed by another and, typically, consultants are too busy to pass on their knowledge to their inexperienced colleagues. As soon as they resolve an issue, or configure something, they move on to the next task or issue. Therefore, throughout the project, consultants transfer very little knowledge to their colleagues—the client's employees.

Repercussions of knowledge transfer failure

Typically, only a small percentage of the company employees working on the project team gain in-depth knowledge about the methods and techniques used to implement SAP™ R/3® software at their site. Consequently, as soon as the consultants leave, there develops a big knowledge gap. This can be avoided if knowledge transfer occurs effectively. Knowledge transfer helps a company retain control over operations as well as future enhancements. Without it, a company's business can become very vulnerable in case of production problems or if, in future, it needs to implement changes or enhancements that require system, process and/or configuration changes.

Ensuring knowledge transfer

The ideal way to ensure knowledge transfer is to force the consultants to allocate time on a consistent basis, throughout the project life, to specific individuals who are identified for this purpose. This task consumes valuable time, which can be spent elsewhere on important project tasks. However, for the long-term benefit, this compromise is essential. Otherwise, the company opens itself up to serious problems in the future.

Effective communication
Working in close proximity

SAP is a team project. The need for effective communication between teams, and with others within the company, is very high. To ensure good communication between the team members, who are drawn from many departments and may never have worked together previously, they should be located within the same area (floor or building). A common characteristic of such an area, for many SAP projects, is that all cubicle partition walls are either removed or decreased in height. Common meeting and lab areas are setup for informal and impromptu meetings or for demos to small groups. This layout architecture, while decreasing privacy, ensures good communication between team members.

Promoting communication

Communication about project status, impending changes, training announcements, rumors, etc., needs to be provided to the company employees on a regular basis. There are many ways in which good communication can be promoted, internally and externally, such as:

- Weekly team meeting where team and project status updates are provided
- Postings on the company intranet
- Newsletters, flyers and e-mails
- Formal and informal information sessions
- Announcements through normal company channels
- Meetings for team building

Chapter 14
Tips for success

What should be done

Obtain commitment

SAP is a team project that can only succeed if it has the backing of key stakeholders. They, along with executive management, should provide the commitment necessary to make the project succeed. Commitment to the goals, objectives and project plan is necessary. If the project plan is not committed to, the project will experience problems due to many issues, such as unavailability of resources, at critical times and may even fail.

Start moving quickly

Time is of the essence in an SAP project. While project tasks are spread out over several months, some decisions need to be made, and tasks are required to be performed, as early as possible. The benefits of doing this include the ability to:

- Identify key users who can make important decisions and influence buy-in
- Mobilize important resources quickly, when required
- Better understand the existing business processes and practices
- Perform data cleanup and validation quickly and efficiently
- Validate new processes

Be prepared

An SAP project is not easy and can spring many surprises at every stage. But there are not too many surprises for those who are prepared. A number of methods can be used to try and be prepared. These include, but are not limited to, the following:

- Create a detailed project plan and publish it in a timely manner
- Work plan should have concrete deliverables with realistic due dates
- Work plan should be adhered to
- Set milestones and enforce them
- Track progress with a forward looking focus: focus on what is coming due
- Project controls and procedures should be effective
- Ensure accountability; make project team members, and others working part-time on the project, responsible for specific tasks
- Expect stealth resource drainers such as reports and customized functionality
- Prepare job descriptions/task definitions well before training commences
- Inform users that initial operations may not be smooth and that the pain could last 3-4 months
- Publicize the fact that implementation will be painful
- Prepare management to expect only minimal financial benefits during the first year

Build team and end-user commitment

For this objective to be achieved, management needs to be proactive. It can help by assigning high priority to project goals and communicating them throughout the organization. Some of the steps that management can take to obtain commitment and enhance performance include:

- Selecting team members with a positive attitude
- Linking project performance, such as meeting milestones, with performance review
- Specifying individual and team accountability
- Imparting a feeling of ownership
- Clearly establishing time commitments
- Identifying resources early; providing commitment to mobilize extra resources, if required
- Making unequivocal public announcement of commitment to the go-live date
- Involving end-users in developing procedures

Create and maintain enthusiasm for the project

An enthusiastic and motivated team is required to implement SAP. However, it is difficult to maintain a high level of enthusiasm throughout the course of an SAP project due to its lengthy duration. Most team members have never been previously exposed to a project of this size and duration. Therefore, many of them are surprised to find out that they have to work so hard, and have to meet high expectations, for a very lengthy period.

On the other hand, for the experienced consultants, this can be another ordinary project in a long line of projects that they have been exposed to. Another negative factor is that the workload for individual team members is cyclical, which can cause them to lose focus and momentum. Therefore, there is a dual requirement that comes into play:

- Create enthusiasm and motivation
- Maintain enthusiasm

A number of steps can be taken to motivate team members. These include:
- Install sense of ownership, which is achieved by involvement, from the beginning of the project
- Provide challenges throughout the duration of the project, which can sustain enthusiasm and commitment
- Do not prolong the decision making process, without rushing into premature decisions, as it can frustrate those who are waiting to proceed
- Set high performance standards for implementation team members

Solve problems in a timely and effective manner

SAP implementation is equivalent to a re-engineering effort during which many important, and critical, decisions need to be made. In many cases, there are conflicts between the different teams and even between team members. These can prevent timely decision-making. Therefore, a mechanism must be put in place for conflict resolution and solving problems in a timely manner.

Some of the steps that can be taken to prevent problems from getting out of hand, and be solved quickly, include the following:
- Assign owners to all issues and problems; clearly define a feedback process that keeps owners in the loop
- Include all concerned in the problem solving and decision making process
- Identify the root cause of the problem
- Issues should not be allowed to drag on; escalate if required
- When a decision is made, document the decision and who made it

Understand what can cause budget overruns

Since ERP projects are huge, even a few oversights while planning and budgeting can make costs spiral out of control. These budget overruns are fairly common and need to be anticipated and controlled.

Who should estimate costs

To avoid getting hit with unexpected expenses, costs should be identified upfront by cross-functional teams assembled for this purpose. These teams can be used to question and/or challenge the other teams' numbers, calculations and assumptions made while budgeting. Such teams should include senior executives, IT personnel, members of other functional groups, and ERP vendor representatives. The inclusion of so many groups can enable a more realistic budget to be prepared.

Controlling costs

Costs need to be controlled for all project tasks. Pressure should be applied for that purpose because a task completed within a budgeted project cost is invariably on time. An area that needs attention is sizing because it can impact everything negatively, especially costs, if not done properly to start with.

Contingency

Budget consciousness needs to be highly stressed. When budgeting, it should be ensured that there is a contingency built in, which can be based on various criteria. However, while contingency should be applied where needed, there should be a penalty associated with using it up.

Areas to watch

The following are the areas that have the potential to contribute to budget overruns significantly:

- ❏ Scope creep
- ❏ Excessive customization
- ❏ Under-estimation of training requirements
- ❏ Ballooning of reporting needs

In many projects, during the past few years, companies have integrated the SAP system with a data warehouse. In such types of projects, a significant amount of analysis needs to be performed on the SAP side to identify the data sources required for populating the data warehouse. This task has typically been underestimated and, consequently, led to cost overruns.

Build appreciation for inter-dependence

In the pre-ERP world, it is fairly common for people to work in individual or small group silos, which changes during SAP implementations. Groups impact each other at every step of the project. The impact of any mistake becomes apparent fairly quickly. Therefore, it is very important that:

- ❏ Team members are made to appreciate inter-dependence
- ❏ Cross-functional communication is improved
- ❏ Team coordination is improved and lone ranger efforts are discouraged
- ❏ Team building efforts are undertaken

Emphasize thorough and effective testing

Testing is a long, but necessary, procedure that is critical to the success of SAP implementations. Both unit and integration testing should be conducted very thoroughly. Testing should be based on a documented plan which must specify the procedures to be followed for testing, bugs resolution, fixing broken processes, regression testing, etc. Some of the steps that can be followed to make testing smooth and successful include the following:

- Select the right people for integration testing; they should be very thorough, detail oriented, and be able to withstand a high pressure environment
- Functional users should be heavily involved, especially during integration testing
- Playback demos, for the benefit of users, should be conducted regularly during the course of the project
- Test scenarios should be created, or reviewed, by business process stakeholders
- Integration test scenarios should be robust and encompass all processes, systems, reports and scenarios; workarounds should not be permitted
- Perform integration testing in a stable environment; do not test while the development effort is still under way
- Do not combine integration testing and training

Start data migration early on

The development effort on the legacy side, for the data migration effort, is handled by the client's own legacy developers because they are more familiar with their own systems. The initial effort, which requires extensive field-to-field mapping from the legacy systems to SAP, is spearheaded by the legacy developers. This task should be started as early as possible. Development effort on the SAP side, which requires knowledge of ABAP™ programming, is handled by ABAP™ developers who, typically, are contractors or employees of the integrator.

Most of the data required to be migrated from the legacy systems to the new SAP system is typically loaded a few days, and sometimes a few weeks, before going live. However, the actual data migration effort usually starts months earlier. There are exceptions like the company that started its data migration effort just a few weeks before going live.

The first test of a data load can be conducted during the simulation phase. This timing is recommended even though only basic configuration may have been done by then. The reason is that experimental data loads highlight issues early on and make the developers more experienced in data loading techniques. This experience can be very valuable when the final data load, into the production client, is undertaken just before go-live. It is highly recommended that at least two or three test loads be undertaken prior to go-live.

A factor that can impact the smoothness and success of the data migration effort is the comprehensiveness and quality of the cutover plan. It should be ensured that this plan is detailed as well as realistic.

Create thorough documentation
Training budget pruning

In the rush to get the system up and running, documentation gets less attention than it deserves. It is one of the first areas to get pruned when there is a budget overrun. It is typical for documentation quality to be sub-standard in delayed projects because, as expected, the time and budget allocated for creating end-user documentation gets reduced.

Understanding documentation needs

For end-users, there are usually two types of documents that need to be rolled out. The first one is customized end-user documentation based on functional areas and job roles. The second one is the business process procedures (BPPs). Besides being used as reference materials, they can be used for training end-users—if it is decided that customized documentation will not be created for them.

System reference documentation

Documenting changes made to the SAP system during the customization process is extremely important. The reason is that consultants ultimately leave the project and, consequently, the knowledge gained during implementation is lost unless there exists adequate documentation. Lack of this documentation can, in some cases, cause serious problems in the future.

Ensuring successful documentation

The following are some tips for ensuring that efficient and thorough documentation is created:

- ❏ Decide the purpose and type of documentation to be created
- ❏ Take a systematic approach for creating documentation; for example: have a shared repository, adopt naming conventions, use templates, etc.
- ❏ Handle creating documentation as a project task, with assigned deliverables, for which specific individuals will be held accountable
- ❏ Provide adequate time in the project plan for documentation
- ❏ Force all team members to document all configuration changes, specifications, enhancements, etc.
- ❏ Coordinate the documentation effort with training
- ❏ Avoid having documentation redundancies and variations

What should not be done

Do not favor technology over business

SAP is a business solution—not a technology project. The reason why businesses buy software is to improve business processes and functions—not because they want to buy data processing technology. An ERP system should not be an IT project because the end-users belong to other departments.

While the importance of technology cannot be minimized, since it prepares for the company's future needs, leading edge technology is often unnecessary and too expensive. This is borne out by the success of SAP™ R/3® software, which is based on mainstream relational database and client/server technology that is more than a quarter century old. While older technology risks becoming obsolete sooner, state-of-the-art technology can be unstable and risky. Therefore, a trade-off between stable and proven technology against new technology is required when evaluating an ERP project.

Do not place functionality requirements on the back seat

The key to a productive new system is functionality. If functionality requirements and user expectations are not met, they will react negatively and become disenchanted. Therefore, one of the first steps in an ERP project should be to determine the desired functions. Once the functions have been identified, the system to be implemented must be able to support them. The implemented system also needs to provide the required functionality with flexibility. If it fails to do so, it can become unproductive.

Avoid duplicating old business processes

The tendency to duplicate existing processes should be discouraged. While it allows a much faster implementation because the approval and signoff process is faster, the end result is that the company will retain its existing inefficient processes and issues. The aim should be to implement best business practices rather than on configuring processes that most closely match the existing processes.

Do not ignore scope creep

One of the biggest problems with SAP projects is the inability to manage scope. As projects increase in scope , the odds of achieving success decreases significantly. In ERP projects, slowly but surely, more and more requirements pile up due to various reasons that, if implemented, result in scope creep. This requires that a balance be struck between satisfying everyone's functionality requirements and the need to control implementation cost and limit risk to the project.

Do not ignore risks

Every software project has risks associated with it and ERP projects are no exception. The risk that these projects face need to be identified and prepared for. The basic risks concern time, budget and planned functionality. The following are some tips for identifying and managing risk:

- Make business objectives the primary drivers of the project
- Do things for the right reasons—for project objectives instead of politics
- Best hedge against risk is to use a proven methodology
- Have tight project controls
- Have realistic milestones and do not change them; make it known that missed deadlines will be penalized
- Realize that high risk exists with existing applications that are retained
- Contingency planning is absolutely necessary
- Make functional managers take ownership and make them accountable
- Communicate a message to those associated with the project that their future success at the company is dependent on a successful implementation
- Do not over customize

Do not modify the system unless necessary

Lesser the number of modifications made to the SAP system, greater are the chances of success. However, if no modifications are made, the systems will perform very well but it may fail to support the business. Therefore, every modification request should be carefully evaluated and approved, or rejected, after considering all the pros and cons.

Avoid changing standard R/3™ objects as much as possible

Ideally, SAP™ R/3® software should be implemented with very few modifications. However, each business is unique and, therefore, SAP needs to be modified and customized so that it can support the business. Many of the requirements can be implemented through configuration changes that modify the database table contents. However, more drastic modifications, such as changing table structures, objects and source code, should not be implemented unless there is a business necessity. The disadvantages of implementing these major changes include:

- Increase in risk
- Increase in cost during implementation as well as upgrades
- Increase in testing requirements
- Additional work is required for every software upgrade and release

Do not start development until requirements have been established

It is not uncommon to initiate development of enhancements, reports, forms, etc., without having the specifications in place. This results in change requests that are unnecessary and expensive. By having specs defined before development starts, the number of iterations required to complete the development are reduced.

It should be a part of the development process to have document sign-off on design specifications. This can prevent, or reduce, surprises being sprung by requestors. It is advisable to complete the design walk-through prior to beginning the programming effort.

Do not be bypassed

Consultants do not know a company's business as well as its employees. They should not be allowed to take over, especially during the requirements gathering (blueprint) phase. Employees should not let themselves be used for rubber stamping decisions. Key company employees should become co-pilots and fully participate in the decision making process.

The primary reason that consultants have been able to proceed in a certain direction, even though that path may not have been in the best interest of the company, is that usually there are no SAP experienced company employees on the project team. Therefore, when the project team is assembled, try to hire a few SAP experienced employees for the project team. Besides being able to question and/or challenge the consultants, if and when required, such employees can form the nucleus of the post go-live SAP organization.

Do not let consultants loose

Always remember that consultants are not the company's own employees. They will not have any on-going benefits from the implementation. However, this does not mean that the advice of consultants should be ignored or dismissed. They provide a very valuable service by filling gaps, providing expertise, and thinking outside the box. They are specialized and can usually work faster and more efficiently. In many cases, they can be invaluable in implementing a successful system. However, it is imperative that their limitations be kept in mind. When working with consultants, keep the following tips in mind:

- ❏ Consultants are not the key for success
- ❏ Monitor consultants closely; do not rely on them to control their costs
- ❏ Maintain full responsibility for those who work on the project and how much they bill
- ❏ Hold consultants accountable; however, they should not be made the scapegoat or given credit for project success
- ❏ Realize that foreign consultants have limited knowledge of country-specific details

Do not underestimate end-user training needs

The proof of the pudding is in the eating. Even if the best SAP system has been implemented, it is useless if the end-users cannot use it easily or effectively. Before they can use it, end-users need to be adequately trained. For most users, the change from the legacy system to the SAP system is drastic and stressful. Therefore, the needs of these end-users should be carefully determined and the training plan created as per their identified needs.

Do not ignore warning signs from partners

Having good partners is an important ingredient for a successful project. On the flip side, a partner that is unresponsive to the client's needs can be a drag on the project. Immediate action needs to be taken if it becomes apparent that a partner does not commit to project scope, milestones and deadlines. Another warning sign is the unwillingness of a partner to allow the client to screen, or let go, a consultant.

Common mistakes and pitfalls

There are a number of common mistakes that are repeated at various SAP implementations. These include, but are not limited, to the following:

Approach and analysis

- ❏ Not realizing that SAP is a political project whose scope equals re-engineering
- ❏ Believing that a flawed business strategy and inefficient business processes can be offset by technology
- ❏ Requirements gathering is over-extended
- ❏ Relaxing too early: not realizing that derailment can occur at any time during any phase

Planning and control
- ❑ Detailed project plan is not created or followed
- ❑ Having loose change control procedures

Team leadership and characteristics
- ❑ Lack of leadership: co-project manger from company's side is weak
- ❑ Weak or dead wood functional team leaders
- ❑ Poor selection of project team members

Scope
- ❑ Lack of scope control; unable to differentiate between want and need
- ❑ Many resource draining stealth projects

Data migration
- ❑ Data cleanup effort is not given sufficient importance
- ❑ Starting the data migration effort too late

Development and testing
- ❑ Starting reports development too late
- ❑ Inadequate testing
- ❑ Starting integration testing before development is complete

Ownership and involvement
- ❑ Lack of ownership
- ❑ Business users are not involved adequately or they hijack the process

Customization

- Attempt to mirror the retiring systems in the new system
- Excessive customization
- Building in lack of flexibility in order to accommodate process

Consulting

- Turnover of consultants is high and takes place at critical junctures
- Not realizing that all consultants do not have the same skills, capabilities and motivation

Communication and training

- Having unrealistic expectations of the software
- End-users are not trained adequately or on time
- Poor communication across the enterprise

Chapter 15
Influence of the marketplace on SAP

Future ERP growth expectations

ERP market growth rate

SAP was initially targeted towards the Fortune 500 companies. As that market saturated, it shifted its focus to the mid-cap market. In order to continue growth, SAP is now targeting even smaller companies—those in the 100 million dollar range. It is also moving away from the rigid client/server approach to a web-enabled front-end, through release 4.6, in response to customer demands for easy, convenient and fast access to data.

Despite the thousands of installations that have been implemented so far, the market for ERP remains quite healthy. AMR Research has estimated that the core ERP market, whose growth rate has been falling, will grow to $21.4 billion in 2004, up from $16.8 in 1999. However, ERP vendors will find high growth opportunities in other areas such as e-business relationship management (ERM), supply chain management and e-Commerce markets. It is estimated that these areas will grow from this $1.6 billion in 1999 to $15.9 billion in 2004.

The following table, based on AMR projections, shows the estimated decline of core ERP applications compared to ERM, supply chain management and e-Commerce applications from 1999 through 2004[14]:

---

[14]EC World, December 2000, pg 79

ERP total revenue by application Percent (estimated)			
Year	Core ERP	Supply chain	ERM	e-Commerce
1999	91	3	4	2
2004	57	15	14	14

SAP growth drivers

In the past, most SAP implementations were for new installations. In the future, we can expect more and more companies with installed SAP systems to extend SAP functionality to their:

❏ Groups/departments/users who were not included in the initial implementation
❏ Subsidiaries and other divisions

Another driver is ERP-to-ERP integration. It is expected that there will be a big push by companies to improve and extend integration by linking with customers and vendors who already use SAP. In the future, we can also expect to see increased customer demand for implementing additional functionality. This will be widespread at companies that initially implemented a vanilla SAP version due to the project requirements for getting the SAP system up and running with only minor modifications to the software.

Drivers for change

In the market that has matured for ERP, customers now demand a more comprehensive solution that extends the core functionality of vendor products beyond traditional ERP, which was limited to automating

the internal processes of companies. Customer demand, to a very large extent, has been influenced by the following four drivers:
- Internet
- Supply chain management
- Customer relationship management
- e-Commerce

Internet

The Internet has been revolutionary. It has fundamentally changed the way many businesses, large and small, are run. SAP has not been untouched by the winds of change. It was somewhat late in recognizing the impact that the Internet would have on its business. However, after SAP realized that it would need to operate in Internet time, it shifted gears and web-enabled the R/3™ software.

Supply chain management (SCM)

SAP integrates a company's various functional areas. However, in order to extend this integration to its partners, suppliers and vendors, additional functionality in the form of supply chain management software is required. SCM manages the flow of products, or services, throughout the processes that typically extend beyond the company to its trading partners.

Previously, a number of independent vendors provided SCM software that was integrated with the SAP™ R/3® software, if SCM functionality was desired by the client.. However, SAP is now trying to incorporate this functionality within its own software. Some of the functionality it has introduced include:
- Advanced Planner and Optimizer™ (SAP APO™), which improves demand-forecasting and increases production efficiency
- Logistics Execution System™ (SAP LES™), which enables efficient, fast and accurate goods flow through the supply chain

This should be a good growth area for SAP in the next few years. Companies interested in this functionality will evaluate SAP as a serious vendor for their needs, even though it is a new entrant in this field, due to its reputation and success in the ERP arena.

Customer relationship management (CRM)

CRM software manages front-end applications, such as sales force automation, in contrast to the back-end which can be managed by the traditional SAP™ R/3® software. In this fast growing market, SAP can manage to grow at a good pace. The competition is tough since other vendors, such as Siebel, are firmly entrenched and have a significant lead. We can expect SAP to incorporate CRM functionality in its core software and attempt to become the preferred, one-stop, vendor of choice.

e-Commerce

This is one of the hottest market sectors at this time. For meaningful e-Commerce, ERP integration with CRM is a critical starting point because companies like to have their front- and back-end software integrated. This reflects the shift in focus from achieving operational efficiency to strategies that are customer-centric and e-Commerce oriented.

Despite its initial mis-steps, SAP is well positioned to make a mark in this area. It is vigorously promoting mySAP.com™ as its e-Commerce portal. We can expect SAP to try and establish itself as a major player in this arena, which is expected to grow very rapidly in the next few years.

SAP's response to the rapidly changing environment

Changes in the ERP market have been fast and significant. Since 1997, SAP has introduced new solutions for customer relationship management, supply chain management and business intelligence. As part of its effort to be responsive to market needs, SAP introduced an Internet-enabled R/3™ in 1996, which was followed by mySAP.com™ in 1999. Some of the new SAP initiatives are discussed in the following sections.

EnjoySAP™

EnjoySAP™, which is R/3™ Release 4.6 with a new graphical interface and featuring full web accessibility, was rolled out in 1999. It aims to adapt the software to each user's requirements. It sports a role-based personal user interface that is visually different than earlier versions. It is easy to use and interactive. It can be easily tailored to individual requirements such as creating favorite lists of the most frequently used transactions. The expected benefits include:

- ❏ 10-65% efficiency improvements for experienced users
- ❏ About 50% reduction in the time required to learn new functions

mySAP.com™

The Internet has been one of the biggest drivers in SAP's evolution during the past few years. Initially, SAP had indicated that it was not going to take the Internet seriously. However, market forces forced SAP to do an about face and web-enable SAP. The result is the latest offering from SAP—mySAP.com™, which provides an open collaborative business environment of personalized solutions on demand.

mySAP.com™ replaces the three-tier architecture foundation with the four-tier architecture, where the 4th component is the web server. mySAP.com™ is based on an open, flexible and scalable Internet architecture. It is the foundation upon which SAP customers can build and execute their Internet and e-business strategies. It supports business-to-business (B2B) and business-to-consumer (B2C) applications. Companies in all types of industries, large and small, can use mySAP.com™ to:

- Become more responsive to their customers' needs and demands
- Bring together their customers, partners and employees
- Facilitate inter-enterprise collaboration
- Gain competitive advantage

mySAP.com™ business application areas are:
- e-Commerce
- Customer relationship management
- Supply chain management
- Strategic enterprise management
- Business intelligence
- Knowledge management
- Human resources
- Logistics execution
- Manufacturing
- Product lifecycle management
- Financials

In the year 2000, mySAP sales accounted for 63% of all SAP software sales—an indication of success in a strategic area[15].

Business intelligence

At most companies, the focus in recent years has shifted, due to the increased competitive environment, from collecting data to using data for decision support. Therefore, instead of relying only on operational (transaction) data, companies now supplement it with data warehouse data, which can be mined with analytical tools, for making informed and sound business decisions.

---
[15]informationweek.com, February 19, 2001, pg 136

SAP reporting limitations

SAP has been extremely good at collecting and storing data. However, it has been limited in its ability to get data out easily and quickly. To be really useful, data needs to be transformed into information, which is required by companies as a competitive weapon. They need specific and accurate information, at the right time, for good decision-making. Without this information, decision-making can be severely impacted and lead to poor business decisions.

Data warehouse solution

Both domestically and internationally, the need to convert data into information is becoming increasingly important. This need for data analysis has caused an explosive growth in data warehousing. The centerpiece of the data warehousing process is the data warehouse, which is a huge data store formatted and optimized for query processing and decision support. It contains data extracted from most of the operational systems of an enterprise.

Data warehouse technology provides the means for extracting data, stored in a company's disparate systems, and transforming it into information that can be used for decision-making. Therefore, the next, if not the parallel, logical step for companies implementing SAP is to implement a data warehouse. With SAP being the most important source of a company's transaction data, it is obvious that data warehouses at SAP installations will obtain their most valuable data from the SAP system.

SAP™ Business Warehouse

Since 1998, SAP has been providing its own data warehouse, which is known as the Business Warehouse (SAP™ BW), as a decision support tool. It contains many pre-defined reporting templates, which include industry-specific functionality.

The most difficult and complicated step in creating a data warehouse is migrating data, extracted and converted from disparate legacy systems, into a single database, i.e., the data warehouse. This task is very tedious and time consuming. When both the SAP transaction system and the SAP™ Business Warehouse are implemented at an installation, the extraction and transformation process is simplified and shortened. The reason is that the transformation routines and other conversion steps, required to migrate data from SAP to the data warehouse (SAP™ BW), are provided by the same vendor—who knows both systems intimately. Therefore, a major task in creating the data warehouse gets simplified.

Ready-to-Run R/3™

This is SAP's pre-configured client, available by vertical market, which targets small- and medium-sized companies. It was released in 1996, with the aim of introducing a system that could be used right out of the box and, consequently, provide both time and cost savings. It is sold as-is, which means that all existing processes need to be discarded in favor of the pre-configured system.

Components

Ready-to-Run R/3™ is a complete solution that includes a pre-installed and pre-configured R/3 system, database, server hardware and operating system. It includes everything that is required to run R/3™ along with the Basis component that is completely pre-configured. All Ready-to-Run R/3™ components are pre-sized and pre-configured to operate in an optimal way. The only requirement is to plug in the system and start operations.

The system includes an online tool, the System Administration Assistant, which specifies the tasks that the system administrator needs to perform on a periodic basis (daily, weekly and monthly).

Features and benefits

Ready-to-Run R/3™ is available in different models, on a number of platforms, for 15-200 users. A customer can choose the model that suits the organization's size and needs. Model selection can be done using a special tool. Ready-to-Run R/3™ contains industry best practices system design and configuration.

Configuration and pre-customization of the R/3™ Basis component is done by experienced consultants and experts drawn from SAP's hardware and database partners. Other advantages associated with Ready-to-Run R/3™ include the following:

- Accelerated R/3™ implementation
- Technical infrastructure can be pre-configured
- Smooth and efficient operation
- Consulting need is limited to data migration and training
- Easy administration: system administrator can perform administrative tasks without first undergoing extensive training
- Cost savings due to easier and faster implementation
- Reduced cost of ownership

Appendix
Evaluating ERP software

Prerequisites for ERP software selection

Basic selection guidelines

Undertaking an ERP project, with its potential for big risks and rewards, can be a daunting task for even the largest companies with deep pockets. If the implementation is successful, it can work wonders for the company while failure can have disastrous consequences. This underscores the necessity for performing a very thorough evaluation before the software is selected and a decision is made to proceed with the proposed project.

The following are the basic guidelines to be used for the evaluation and selection process:
- ❏ Evaluation should be based on facts and be objective
- ❏ A well proven methodology should be used

An evaluation process based on these two criteria enables a well-informed decision that can be easily justified.

Use a proven methodology

An ERP project needs to be approached systematically and methodically. To be successful, such a project needs to be implemented using a structured methodology. An ERP project should not be implemented without a well-proven methodology. With such a tool, risk is reduced and a mechanism is provided to handle unexpected situations and problems. Without it, serious problems can occur including project derailment.

Evaluate the business strategy

Before an ERP software is selected, the company's business strategy needs to be understood. If it is inflexible and does not permit the use of new processes, the selection choices will be reduced. Therefore, it is imperative that the business strategy be determined before embarking on a project of this nature because it is impossible to back out, after the project has started, without serious financial and political repercussions.

Study the business processes

The software needs should be defined based upon the results obtained by analyzing the existing business processes and flows. It should not be done the other way around, i.e., by selecting the software first and then studying the business processes.

The process should be started by comparing the existing business processes and strategies to those supported by the new system (as-is versus to-be). This should be followed by the software selection process and the evaluation of software functions and features. If the functions are evaluated right upfront, without examining the business background and processes, the initial progress is rapid. However, in such a case, the end result may not be what is best, or optimal, for the organization. Therefore, it is advisable to follow a selection process that starts by evaluating the organization's strategy and business processes.

Evaluate the impact of a re-engineering decision

If a company has already made a decision to perform re-engineering, which means redesigning practically everything, it will significantly influence the software evaluation and selection process. While there are advantages to this approach, it has its drawbacks such as:

- ❏ Greater implementation risk
- ❏ Requires complete business process redesign
- ❏ Higher implementation cost
- ❏ Slower deployment
- ❏ Greater configuration complexity

Favor industry-specific templates

Depending on the industry, implementation can be accelerated by the use of industry specific templates, if available and applicable. These templates contain pre-defined best business practices for specific industries.

A vendor able to provide industry-specific templates will start off with an advantage in the evaluation process. SAP has created pre-configured industry-specific templates in partnership with various consulting companies. Using these templates enables simpler and faster deployment. However, because industry-specific best business practices are incorporated in the templates, their use forces companies to make trade-offs and compromises due to reduced flexibility caused by the use of these templates.

It should be realized that templates only cut some initial work off the implementation. Even when they are used, the configuration and processes still need to be verified, at every step, for applicability to the implementation site. When required, such as a situation where a particular process is not supported by the template, appropriate changes need to be implemented.

Involve the business users

An ERP project is not a technology project. It should be owned and driven by the business users. Viewing an ERP system as a technology or software project is one of the surest ways to failure—as has been demonstrated by so many companies. The logic for this is simple. IT does not have the business expertise to evaluate the implications of various trade-offs that need to be made throughout the project—from software evaluation and selection through implementation. It also does not have the capability to evaluate decisions based on their strategic versus operational impact. Those decisions are best left to the business users and their management.

Be wary of proof-of-concept offer

It is fairly common for vendors to propose a proof-of-concept offer. In this scenario, the vendor implements and demonstrates a working model of its software based on the potential client company's business data. These offers should be carefully evaluated before they are accepted. If an offer is accepted, the vendor should be made to demonstrate carefully scripted business scenarios developed by the client's employees.

Be aware of the cost of failure

A successful ERP implementation leads to many benefits for an organization. However, a failed implementation can be very costly in terms of dollars and morale. Due to its vast reach across the enterprise, such a software cannot be easily scrapped after it has been implemented. Also, it can take years before it becomes apparent that an implementation is seriously flawed and that it needs to be scrapped. By the time this is realized, tens of millions of dollars may have been spent. Also, at such a stage, the alternatives are few and, therefore, it is not easy to cut the losses and run. In such cases, the losses can continue to balloon, benefits can be illusionary even after enhancements and rework, and lost opportunities can be significant.

Additional points to ponder

As part of the evaluation process, a company needs to look inwards and study its strengths and weaknesses. The result of this analysis can help in deciding whether or not to implement an ERP system. It can also help in identifying the ERP package that is more suitable for the company. The

two fundamental questions that need to be answered during the evaluation process are:
- How should this business be run
- What are the business problems that the ERP package should address

Other factors to consider include assessing executive sponsorship, priorities, gaps between the existing system and the ERP package, costs and benefits, as well as proposed tasks and schedule. Also to be evaluated are the implementation options:
- Using implementation partners, or
- Using the company's own employees supported by consultants

Finally, two very important factors that also need to be evaluated are the vendor's:
- Internet and e-Commerce strategy
- Supply chain management system offering

Basic selection considerations

Model of doing business

ERP packages are based on business models that may be incompatible or fundamentally different than the way the company does business. To enable implementation when there is incompatibility, either the company has to change the way it conducts its business or the software has to be modified. Both these choices have potentially serious implications that need to be evaluated before making any selection.

Functionality

The first step should be to identify the business problems that need to be addressed. They determine which specific functionality the software package must support. The suitability of a software package can vary considerably depending on where the functionality requirements originate from: Finance, Manufacturing, Human Resources or some other group. For example, the need to integrate financial data has different requirements than those for standardizing production systems across the enterprise.

ERP packages have different features, despite a common base and approach, and some excel in specific areas. Therefore, their suitability for a particular implementation can be dramatically different. This, to some extent, can be attributed to their different evolution paths. For example, some ERP vendors started off by developing manufacturing software while others started off down a completely different path—such as PeopleSoft, whose first module was Human Resources.

Analysis and reporting

The need for reporting varies at different organizational levels. The requirements of top management are quite different compared to a line manager's requirements. Again, management style can vary across organizations. Some like to drill down and look at the lowest level (transactions). Others are only interested in looking at the big picture. Therefore, the ability of the software to provide high-level reporting as well as granular data is a factor to consider during the selection process.

The ease of use in accessing data through standard reports can be a big plus. Also to be considered, when evaluating reporting capabilities, is the current or future availability of an integrated data warehouse that, besides providing better analytical reports, is more user-friendly.

Show stoppers

During the evaluation process, as features are evaluated in-depth, there is a fair chance that a showstopper may be discovered. This can be a business

process that is not supported by the ERP package or it can be a critical piece of missing functionality. The following are examples of showstoppers:
- ❏ Does not support the needs of the company, with international operations, which requires 24x7 support and service
- ❏ Does not support multi-currencies or languages
- ❏ Critical process(es) are unsupported
- ❏ Estimated implementation time is unacceptable

What to do before buying

Evaluate using cross-functional teams

An integrated system must be evaluated by representatives of all major groups—Finance, Manufacturing, Sales, etc. This ensures that functionality and processes are evaluated in all functional areas and, therefore, all bases are covered. This involvement also enables easy buy-in.

Check references and sites

It is always advisable to move beyond the evaluation phase sales pitches. One of the best ways to obtain useful information is to visit sites that have already implemented the ERP package. For example, a semiconductor company evaluating SAP should communicate with, and visit, other semiconductor companies that have already implemented SAP.

It should be realized that more than a few phone calls will be required. It is far more effective to visit an operating site and talk to the personnel closely involved with the implementation and operation at that site. The intelligence gathered during such trips, along with tips and warnings, can ensure that mistakes are not repeated.

Useful information can also be obtained by attending user conferences and events such as the SAPPHIRE® conference. This conference is SAP's annual event where it usually announces new functionality and news. This event is attended by thousands of users and the discussions there, with other participants and SAP experts, can be very useful and informative.

Request onsite demo

The vendor should be asked to demonstrate support for the processes and functionality it seeks to replace. This demo should be based on detailed business scenarios that are created by the various functional groups. The ability to support critical processes can be the basis for allowing the vendor to proceed to the next stage in the evaluation and selection process.

Beware of consultants involved in the selection process

Integrators and consultants are often involved in the evaluation process. Their experience is valuable since they have experienced many implementations. However, at times, they can be less than objective due to a number of reasons. For example, an integrator may be biased towards a particular ERP system because it may be more experienced in that package or most of its benched consultants may be specialized in that ERP package. Therefore, the final decision should be made independently by the company's employees.

Selection nuts and bolts

Selection criteria

In order to implement an ERP package, a company will need to evaluate and select the following:
- Software package
- System integrator (consulting company with implementation expertise)
- Hardware vendor

Every company performing an evaluation, for each of these three items, will have its own screening and selection criteria. The following is a list of variables that, typically, may be used for evaluating an ERP software package:
- Flexibility
- Information access
- Functionality
- Technical environment
- Cost
- Ease of implementation
- Vendor

Depending upon each company's own criteria, additional variables can be added to this list. These variables can be assigned equal or unequal weights during the scoring and ranking process. In the following list, the number within each bracket indicates the weight that was assigned to the variable by a mid-cap company during its ERP selection process.
- Flexibility (20%)
- Information access (20%)
- Functionality (15%)
- Technical environment (15%)
- Cost (10%)
- Ease of implementation (10%)
- Vendor (10%)

The importance of each selection variable will vary from organization to organization. Therefore, the weight that is assigned to each variable will, typically, be different for each implementation.

160 *Implementing SAP*

The following is a list of variables that can be used to select a hardware vendor for an ERP implementation:
- Ability to meet business needs
- Availability of resources
- Non-proprietary: follows open standards
- Level of integration
- Reputation and financial strength of company
- Penetration in vertical market of interest

Scoring and ranking ERP packages

This section demonstrates a method for scoring and ranking three ERP packages, "A", "B" and "C" using five different variables. The objective is to select the most appropriate ERP package. Table 1 lists the five variables that will be used to score and rank the three packages. It also lists the actual values, corresponding to each of the five variables, for all three packages.

#	Variable	Package A	Package B	Package C
	Table 1: Values for ERP selection variables (determined during the evaluation process)			
1.	Cost ($ million)	16	14	16
2.	Functionality/Features	Acceptable	Most	Acceptable
3.	Implementation time (months)	6	12	9
4.	Flexibility	Excellent	Fair	Good
5.	Reporting capability	Fair	Fair	Good

Scoring

Table 2 lists the ERP selection variables and their corresponding scores. For example, if the implementation cost for the package ranges between 15 and 20 million dollars, its score will be 8. For every installation, the scores corresponding to each variable listed in Table 2 will be different. The reason for this is that the importance of each variable varies from company to company.

It should be noted that Table 2 has been constructed with sample data. The value for each data item in Table 2 will, for each implementation, need to be assigned by the evaluation team based on the company's objectives and priorities.

Table 2
ERP selection variables and corresponding scores

No.	Variable	Variable value (X)	Score to be used (Y)
1.	Cost ($million)	10-15	10
		15-20	8
		20-25	6
		>25	4
2.	Functionality/Features	All features	10
		Most	8
		Acceptable	6
		Fair	4
		Show stoppers	0
3.	Implementation time (months)	6	10
		9	8
		12	6
		15	4
		18	2
4.	Flexibility	Excellent	10
		Good	7
		Fair	4
		Poor	1
5.	Reporting capability	Excellent	10
		Good	7
		Fair	4
		Poor	1

Ranking

After the scores have been assigned in Table 2, the packages are ranked in the next step. For this purpose, Tables 3, 4 and 5 are completed, after assigning a weight (W) to each variable to reflect its relative importance to the company, as shown below:

<table>
<tr><td colspan="6" align="center">Table 3
Ranking calculations for package A</td></tr>
<tr><th>No.</th><th>Variable</th><th>Weight
(W)</th><th>Value*
(X)</th><th>Score**
(Y)</th><th>Total Score
(Z=W*Y)</th></tr>
<tr><td>1.</td><td>Cost ($ million)</td><td>10</td><td>16</td><td>8</td><td>80</td></tr>
<tr><td>2.</td><td>Functionality/Features</td><td>9</td><td>Acceptable</td><td>6</td><td>54</td></tr>
<tr><td>3.</td><td>Implementation time</td><td>8</td><td>6</td><td>10</td><td>80</td></tr>
<tr><td>4.</td><td>Flexibility</td><td>5</td><td>Excellent</td><td>10</td><td>50</td></tr>
<tr><td>5.</td><td>Reporting capability</td><td>6</td><td>Fair</td><td>4</td><td>24</td></tr>
<tr><td></td><td>**Grand Total:**</td><td></td><td></td><td></td><td>**288**</td></tr>
<tr><td colspan="6">*   Values obtained from Table 1
** Scores obtained from Table 2</td></tr>
</table>

<table>
<tr><td colspan="6" align="center">Table 4
Ranking calculations for package B</td></tr>
<tr><th>No.</th><th>Variable</th><th>Weight
(W)</th><th>Value*
(X)</th><th>Score**
(Y)</th><th>Total Score
(Z=W*Y)</th></tr>
<tr><td>1.</td><td>Cost ($ million)</td><td>10</td><td>14</td><td>10</td><td>100</td></tr>
<tr><td>2.</td><td>Functionality/Features</td><td>9</td><td>Most</td><td>8</td><td>72</td></tr>
<tr><td>3.</td><td>Implementation time</td><td>8</td><td>12</td><td>6</td><td>48</td></tr>
<tr><td>4.</td><td>Flexibility</td><td>5</td><td>Fair</td><td>4</td><td>20</td></tr>
<tr><td>5.</td><td>Reporting capability</td><td>6</td><td>Fair</td><td>4</td><td>24</td></tr>
<tr><td></td><td>**Grand Total:**</td><td></td><td></td><td></td><td>**264**</td></tr>
<tr><td colspan="6">*   Values obtained from Table 1
** Scores obtained from Table 2</td></tr>
</table>

Table 5
Ranking calculations for package C

No.	Variable	Weight (W)	Value* (X)	Score** (Y)	Total Score (Z=W*Y)
1.	Cost ($ million)	10	16	8	80
2.	Functionality/Features	9	Acceptable	6	54
3.	Implementation time	8	9	8	64
4.	Flexibility	5	Good	7	35
5.	Reporting capability	6	Good	7	42
	Grand Total:				275

* Values obtained from Table 1
** Scores obtained from Table 2

The result of the ranking exercise is:
❑ ERP Package A = 288 points
❑ ERP Package B = 264 points
❑ ERP Package C = 275 points

Therefore, based on this analysis, ERP package "A" should be favored since it scores higher than both packages "B" and "C."

Vendor selection tips

The basic selection requirement for an ERP package is that it must meet the business process and functionality requirements. Another factor that requires serious evaluation, in addition to the other requirements discussed earlier, is the vendor supplying the software package. The following are the sub-criteria for evaluating ERP vendors:

❑ Culture match
❑ Financial stability
❑ Risk associated with the vendor
❑ Vision and strategy

- Credibility
- Relationship with vendor
- References
- Size (small versus big)
- Industry specialization

The weight assigned to this variable can vary depending upon the company culture and other factors. For example, as shown earlier in the "Selection criteria" section, the ERP vendor variable was assigned a 10% weight during the evaluation process at one implementation.

Index

ABAP developers, 90, 131
ABAP/4, 16, 22, 24, 30 ,90
AcceleratedSAP, 11, 51
Advanced Planner and Optimizer, 143
Application layer, 30-31
Application servers, 30-32
ASAP components, 54, 60
ASAP methodology, 11, 13, 53-54
ASAP partner, 52, 54
ASAP Roadmap, 52, 57, 58, 76
As-is, 49, 148, 152
Authorization(s), 6, 30, 58, 100, 102, 103
Baan, 3, 12
Benchmark, 11
Best business practices, 5, 19, 21, 42, 52, 55, 134, 153
Budget overruns, 129
Business Blueprint, 58-59, 70, 76, 118
Business drivers, 65, 111
Business Engineer, 55-56, 76
Business navigator, 55
Business process procedures (BPP), 78, 132
Business processes, 1, 5, 18, 30, 41-42, 47, 49, 54-58, 64, 68, 71-73, 76, 78-79, 96, 100, 116, 125, 133-134, 138, 152
Business Warehouse, 147-148
Business workflow, 24, 30
Business-to-business (B2B), 17, 145

Business-to-consumer (B2C), 145
Change control procedure, 100, 104
Checklists, 52, 57, 59
Client, 16, 30-31, 34-36, 66-67, 96-97, 100, 119-120, 122, 131-132, 134, 138, 141, 143, 148, 154
Client architecture, 119-120
Client refresh strategy, 119
Client/server, 16, 30, 31, 134, 141
Collaborative enterprise solutions, 16
Communication, 16, 100-101, 115, 123, 130, 140, 169
Company code, 35, 74
Consultants, 21-23, 38, 40, 52-54, 56, 66-69, 71, 76-77, 96-97, 104, 108-109, 115, 117, 122-123, 127, 132, 136-137, 140, 149, 155, 158
Consulting costs, 11
Contingency, 129, 135
Conventional methodology, 48, 50, 54
Conversions, 58, 83
Core team, 67, 81-82, 104-105, 167
Corporate culture, 10, 42, 110
Cost center, 74
Cost estimation, 11
Cost per user, 11
Cost savings, 6, 9, 148-149
Cost/benefit, 107
Cross-functional teams, 129, 157
Currencies, 19
Customer loyalty, 18, 65, 112
Customer relationship management, 41, 143-144, 146
Customization, 11, 14, 19, 21-22, 35, 40, 78, 81, 104, 130, 132, 140
Customizing, 21-22, 47, 57
Data archiving, 30
Data cleanup, 83, 86, 92, 121, 125, 139

Data consistency, 19, 31
Data load sequence, 92
Data migration, 35, 70, 84, 88, 91, 97, 119-120, 131-132, 139, 149
Data redundancy, 19
Data structures, 19
Data Warehouse, 130, 146-148, 156, 167
Data Warehousing, 106, 108, 147
Database layer, 30-31
Database servers, 30, 32
Databases, 7, 19, 31, 33
Decentralized architecture, 32
Decision makers, 62, 112
Dirty data, 79, 86
EarlyWatch, 60, 103
Earnings growth, 65
e-business strategies, 145
e-Commerce, 17, 41, 105, 141, 143-144, 146, 155
Effective controls, 117
End-user documentation, 78, 132
Enhancements, 31, 41, 58, 88-89, 100, 104, 118, 122-123, 133, 136, 154
EnjoySAP, 145
Escalation rules, 117-118
Evaluation process, 38, 151, 153-156, 158, 164
Extended team, 67, 121
Final preparation, 59, 91, 93-94, 97-98
Financial benefits, 17, 126
Functional managers, 135
Gap analysis, 47
Going Live check, 60-61, 98
Go-live plan, 91-92
Graphical user interface, 19, 31
Guiding principles, 64, 111

Hershey Foods, 37
IBM, 15, 31, 33, 87
Implementation Assistant, 55, 57
Implementation budget, 93
Implementation cost, 10, 46, 52, 134, 153, 160
Implementation risks, 40, 71
Implementation scope, 40, 71
Independent consultants, 69
Industry-specific templates, 153
Instance, 34-35
Integration testing, 79-81, 88, 91, 99, 117, 119-121, 130-131, 139
Integrators, 40, 158
Inter-company processing, 73
Interfaces, 2-3, 58, 70, 72, 81, 88, 91, 98-99
Internet, 23, 103, 143, 145, 155
Internet training, 23
Inventory reduction, 7
Issues database, 58
JD Edwards, 3
Knowledge corner, 57
Knowledge transfer, 67-68, 77, 91, 96-97, 122-123
Lawson, 3
Level I training, 69, 94
Level II training, 72, 77, 94
Level III training, 94
Life cycle, 5
Logistics Execution System, 143
Mapping, 47, 49, 102, 131
Master data, 31, 35, 72-74, 83, 85, 87, 121
Materials management, 2, 18, 24-25, 29, 80, 167
Materials requirement planning, 2
Meta Group, 9, 12, 17

Metrics, 65, 100, 112
Mid sized companies, 10, 16, 51, 148
Mistakes, 120, 138, 157
Modeling, 47, 55-56
MySAP.com, 16, 144-146
Network infrastructure, 11
Obsolete systems, 4, 18
Operating systems, 7, 19, 33
Oracle, 3, 12, 16-17, 31, 33
Organizational structure, 33, 35, 66, 71-74, 104
OSS, 60, 103
Concept check, 60
PeopleSoft, 3, 156
Performance, 3, 6, 38, 60-61, 65, 79, 97-98, 119, 126-128, 167
Performance tests, 97-98
Physical architecture, 30, 35
Pitfalls, 110, 138
Plant capacity, 7
Plants, 72, 75
Platform, 43
Playbacks, 77
Productivity improvements, 7
Profit center, 26, 74
Profitability, 18, 26, 43, 65, 112
Profitability growth, 18, 65, 112
Project Estimator, 55-56
Project justification, 107
Project manager, 65, 109, 111, 113, 117
Project planning, 62-63, 94, 114
Project principles, 106
Project risk, 110
Project team characteristics, 116

Proof-of-concept, 154
Purchase orders, 7, 80, 83
Purchasing organization, 75
Quality Assurance, 34, 60, 68, 82, 167
Questionnaires, 52, 54
R/3 objects, 136
R/3 Reference model, 54
Ranking, 159-160, 162-163
Readiness assessment, 99, 108
Realization, 51, 59, 76, 78, 94
Re-engineering, 11, 42, 50, 53, 114, 128, 138, 152
Regression testing, 121, 130
Releases, 41, 45, 103
Reporting, 6, 44, 72-73, 83, 89, 130, 147, 156
Reports, 6, 34, 43-44, 58, 86, 88-90, 99-100, 118-119, 126, 131, 136, 139, 156
Resource availability, 7
Return on investment (ROI), 7, 56
Roadmap, 46, 52, 57-59, 76, 108
Sales and distribution, 2, 24, 29, 68
Sales organization, 75
SAP growth drivers, 142
SAP Procedure model, 48-49
SAP R/2, 16
SAP R/3 software, 16, 18, 22, 23, 24, 34, 38, 39, 47, 64, 69, 71, 73, 76, 81, 83, 102, 104, 108, 122, 133, 136, 143, 144
SAPNet, 103
Scope, 9, 11-12, 40, 46-47, 49, 53, 56-57, 66, 70-71, 88, 91, 94, 101, 107, 109, 113, 117-119, 130, 134, 138-139
Scope creep, 117-119, 130, 134
Scoping, 47
Scoring, 159-160
Security, 6, 44, 102-103

Selection considerations, 155
Selection criteria, 158-159, 164
Setting rules, 118
Showstoppers, 99, 157
Simulation, 59, 76, 132
Skill sets, 43, 68
Small sized companies, 16
Software cost, 11
Software release, 22
SQL, 31, 33
SQL Server, 33
Staffing, 104-105
Steering Committee, 66, 93, 101, 112-113, 118
Strategic business objectives, 107-108
Strategic guiding principles, 64
Stress tests, 98
Supply chain, 7, 41, 108, 141, 143-144, 146, 155
System administration, 68, 91, 97, 148-149
System integrator, 158
System Software Associates, 3
Team building, 69, 124, 130
Team characteristics, 68, 116
TeamSAP, 22-23
Technical guides, 52
Testing process, 81
To-be, 47, 49, 76, 152
Total cost of ownership, 12
Training, 15, 23, 27, 34, 52-53, 68-69, 72, 77-78, 91, 93-96, 100-103, 115, 117, 123, 126, 130-133, 138, 140, 149, 167
Training fees, 53
Training materials, 95-96
Transaction data, 31, 35, 72, 83, 85-87, 121, 146-147

Transition ability, 109
Transport(s), 30, 100, 119
Unisource Worldwide, 37
Unit testing, 80
Upgrade cycle, 104
Upgrades, 4, 14, 45, 136
Validation, 59, 78, 83, 87, 92, 125
Validity checks, 6, 44
Vendor selection, 163

About the Author

Arshad Khan is a versatile professional, consultant, an adjunct professor, and an established author. His IT experience includes many Data Warehouse and SAP full life-cycle implementations. Mr. Khan, who started his SAP career in 1995, has worked in many roles during various SAP implementations. These include Team Lead for manufacturing (Production Planning, Materials Management and Quality Management modules), Technical Training Manager, Solutions Specialist, Core Team member and Quality Assurance team member. He has worked for many well-known companies including LSI Logic Corporation, Acuson Corporation and Hitachi America.

Mr. Khan has written books in diverse fields including software implementation, chemical engineering (desalination), stock market investing and performance improvement. His first book, published by Elsevier Science Publishers (Reed) in 1986, was awarded the first prize for the best engineering book.

Mr. Khan has taught a variety of courses at the University of California (Berkeley and Santa Cruz Extensions), Golden Gate University and National University since 1988. Besides various information technology and investment courses, he has also taught "Implementing SAP projects," "Understanding SAP" and "Materials Management". Mr. Khan has a graduate degree in engineering as well as an MBA.

0-595-23398-8

Printed in Great Britain
by Amazon.co.uk, Ltd.,
Marston Gate.